Accessing Aidan

The story of the Bamburgh Ossuary

ISBN No: 978-1-873402-27-6

Design and print by Printspot, Berwick-upon-Tweed

Contents

AD 604   Oswald born, son of Aethelfrith Ruler of Bernicia and Acha of Deira

AD 616   Aethelfrith killed in battle, Acha's brother Edwin became King – Acha went into exile with her five children in Iona. The conversion of Oswald and his brothers to Celtic Christianity at St Columba's monastery began

AD 633   Edwin killed in battle

AD 634   The Battle of Heavenfield (Hexham) between Oswald and Cadwallon. Upon his victory Oswald united the kingdoms of Bernicia and Deira to form Northumbria with the main royal court based at Bamburgh

AD 635   Aidan summoned by Oswald to help convert Northumbria to Christianity, Oswald gave Aidan the island of Lindisfarne to found his monastery

AD 642   Oswald killed at the Battle of Maserfield by the pagan Penda of Mercia

AD 651   Aidan died – leaning against his timber church at Bamburgh – the beam above the vestry is reputed to be the timber he leant on

AD 664   The Synod of Whitby

AD 665   Cuthbert became the Bishop of Lindisfarne

AD 687   Death of Cuthbert

AD 793   Vikings raided Lindisfarne

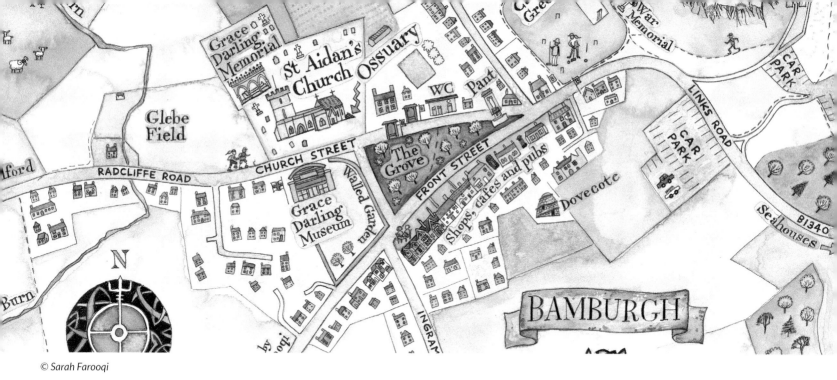

Introduction

In 2016 St. Aidan's Parochial Church Council together with Bamburgh Heritage Trust found themselves in the extraordinary position of creating a brand new ossuary in the crypt of St Aidan's Church, Bamburgh for over 100 Anglo-Saxon skeletons.
This book explores a series of fascinating stories of our Anglo-Saxon ancestors as well as the remarkable circumstance and characters that resulted in the Bamburgh Ossuary.

Ossuary:
noun /ˈɒs.jʊə.riˀ/ a place or container where the bones of dead people are kept
ORIGIN OF OSSUARY
1650-60 < Late Latin *ossuarium*, variant of *ossarium*, equivalent ot oss- (stem of os)
+ -*arium* -ary.

Ossuaries, also sometimes known as Charnel Houses (charnel - the origins of the word is early medieval and derives from the Latin *carnāle* 'carnal' meaning *of the flesh*), were actually a common feature of the medieval ecclesiastical landscape and are still commonplace in some catholic countries of continental Europe. The creation of church ossuaries dates from the mid 12th century. In Britian 'charnelling' or the creation of ossuaries was one of the more catholic traditions that fell out of favour during the 16th century Reformation and the architecture associated with it was quickly abandoned or repurposed. Pages 78-86 explore ossuaries more fully.

Between 1999 and 2007 the Bamburgh Research Project excavated an Anglo-Saxon burial site from beneath the sand dunes to the south of Bamburgh Castle in an area known as the Bowl Hole. In total the remains of over 120 skeletons were excavated. 98 of these are identifiable discrete burials and feature in the digital Bamburgh Ossuary. The extensive osteological study of the skeletons was conducted by Durham University under the direction of Prof. Charlotte Roberts and was completed in 2012.

As all professional archaeologists know the excavation of human remains is done under licence from the Ministry of Justice and the licence stipulates the reburial or deposition of the remains in an appropriate way. In the instance of the Bowl Hole skeletons the licence stipulated reburial. The natural environment protection designations that cover the Bamburgh sand dunes coupled with the dynamic nature of the dunes themselves and the potential for other buried archaeological deposits dictated that reburial on site was not practical. So whilst a different reburial solution was sought the skeletons, in archaeological acid free boxes, rested in a discrete side room off one of the public rooms in Bamburgh Castle.

Around the same time as the osteological research was completed a small community group was formed in Bamburgh - Bamburgh Heritage Trust - to celebrate the amazing wealth and depth of heritage of the village and surrounding area. The driving force behind the Trust were Jude Aldred and the Trust's chair the Revd Canon Brian Hurst. It was whilst exploring potential village locations for heritage interpretation that Brian first mentioned the crypt of St. Aidans. By 2016 the residents of Bamburgh had come to see these people buried in the dunes as their Anglo-Saxon ancestors. The close tangible link to the northern saints - St. Aidan and St.

Oswald - dictated that this early Christain congregation deserved a special reburial.

The skeletons were interred into crypt, their final resting place, on Friday 24th June 2016. Each skeleton placed in their own zinc ossuary box.

The creation of the Bamburgh Ossuary proved the inspiration for the Accessing Aidan project – the project name was chosen to reflect the desire to make the crypt and the stories of those people resting there accessible both phsyically and intellectually. In early 2018 the National Lottery Heritage Fund awarded a grant to a partnership of St. Aidan's Parochial Church Council, the Northumberland Coast AONB and Bamburgh Heritage Trust supported by Bamburgh Research Project and Durham University. This grant and contributions from other funders enabled the crypt to be opened to the public, create a digital ossuary and interpret the remarkable Anglo-Saxon story. And from Accessing Aidan came Bamburgh Bones – the website and digital ossuary.

Ossuary boxes in the Bamburgh Ossuary
© Andy Garrdner Website Design

A personal note from the Project Officer:

For the last three years it has been my privilege to be the project officer for the Accessing Aidan/Bamburgh Bones project – a National Lottery Heritage Funded project to interpret the remarkable Anglo-Saxon heritage of Bamburgh focusing on the Bamburgh Ossusary in the crypt of St. Aidan's Church. Working in partnership with a wealth of brilliant volunteers, the fabulous community and church together with professional archaeologists from Bamburgh Research Project and Durham University has been one of the most rewarding experiences of my working life. I've learnt so much, met many brilliant people and enjoyed every moment.

Accessing Aidan came about because a community recognised that they had a fascinating story to tell. The good people of Bamburgh are rightly proud of their remarkable Anglo-Saxon ancestors whose endeavour and adventure resulted in the creation of the cosmopolitan cultural capital of Britain 1400 years ago. This Anglo-Saxon population have taught us that migration is nothing new, that we should not fear it but welcome and embrace the cultural traditions of all people and aspire to a new Golden Age.

Much of what we know about the reign of King Oswald and the teaching of the gentle saintly Aidan come from the writings of the Venerable Bede. Bede was writing from the perspective of the Roman Catholic church, and it is therefore unsurprising that women are not readily prominent in his narrative of Anglo-Saxon Britain. But our present-day journey to celebrate that history is dominated by some remarkable and brilliant women.

First amongst them was Jude Aldred – no words can adequately express just how wonderful this woman was. She was instrumental in setting up Bamburgh Heritage Trust and she was the driving force behind this project and the creation of the ossuary. She was so proud of her wonderful Bamburgh heritage and everything she did was for the love of this wonderful village and the north Northumbrian culture. She travelled the world and had her share of adventure, but her love of this place eventually brought her and daughter Kate home. We spent so many funny happy hours drinking tea and plotting at her kitchen table.

On the 18th June 2018 Jude passed away – she was a formidable woman and fabulous friend. Her loss was and is still devastating. And it was for her and in her memory that the project carried on and was completed.

Rest in Peace Jude.

Jessica Turner

Ossuary box detail
© Andy Gardner Web Design

The Archaeology of the Bowl Hole

Graeme Young

Graeme Young is one of the directors of the Bamburgh Research Project Ltd which is dedicated to the archaeological investigation Bamburgh and its environs. He lives in Northumberland and has worked in archaeology for 34 years and been with the BRP since 1996. Whilst something of an archaeological all-rounder he has a special interest in the early medieval period.

Bamburgh Castle and dunes
© Andy Gardner Web Design

Introduction

A huge storm beating down on an exposed coastline, with winds so strong, sand that had lain for centuries, was stripped away to reveal long lost human burials...it does rather sound like the beginning of an adventure novel, and one that was more than a little fanciful. How extraordinary then that that this is the beginning of our tale of investigation and discovery and it is all quite true. We may need to use our imagination a little in order to fill in the inevitable gaps and paint a vivid picture of the past, but even so we can stick to what the evidence tells us and still have an enthralling story that opens a window into lives lived more than 1300 years ago, and who were visitors to, or members of, a long lost Kingdom.

Whatever caused the storm that revealed them the great storm occurred in the winter of 1817. Its results are first recorded by an Antiquarian called MacKenzie writing in 1826. He tells us that the winds stripped the sand from an ancient burial ground that lay some 200 to 300m to the south of the gatehouse at Bamburgh Castle in Northumberland. It is just possible that this great storm was one of the results of a massive volcanic eruption in the Far East. The eruption of Tambora volcano was one of the biggest ever recorded, throwing some 160-213 cubic kilometres of material into the atmosphere. 1816 was known as the year without a summer when temperatures plummeted and crops failed after heavy rain! The following winters were grim and temperatures did not recover for a few years.

Many of the graves of the ancient burial ground were notable for being outlined by slate flagstones, set on edge, to form what are called *cists*. These were seen over an extensive area of around 1000m square, and appeared to represent only a part of the cemetery as this ground surface extended further than the area revealed by the storm. Much, it seemed, still awaited discovery beneath this complex dune system. These burials were explored by antiquarians from the 19th century and up to the middle of the 20th century, but sadly the current research team have not been able to find any drawings or records of this work that could add to our understanding of the site. The location of the cemetery, described on the

Ordnance Survey of around 1860, as 'ancient Danish burial ground', tell us that they thought it Viking in date. Despite this previous investigation and recording by the time that Dr Brian Hope-Taylor came to investigate Bamburgh in 1959, the exact site of the cemetery had been lost and Hope-Taylor placed its rediscovery as one of his objectives. Perhaps influenced by the description of a barrow cemetery in the early medieval epic Beowulf he sited a series of test pits on the high ground overlooking the beach, but none on the exact site noted by the Ordnance Survey. The reporting of human bone fragments from the Bowl Hole itself (a deep hollow in the sand dunes that floods in winter) from a walk over survey undertaken by Northumberland County Council's archaeological team during the 1970s, added to the urgency of its rediscovery. It was assumed that these had been washed into the low ground after being eroded from the cemetery site and therefore must be under threat of slow destruction.

Photo of a cist burial prior to excavation showing the partial stone lining that we see around about one quarter of the graves.
© G. Young

Such was the state of our understanding when the Bamburgh Research Project was set up in 1996, and with the urgency of the erosion risk, we made fixing the cemetery's location - and discovering if it was indeed under threat - a priority. In addition, we had our own questions about its date. Was it really a Viking Age cemetery as labelled on the Ordnance Survey map? There was some scepticism amongst the research team, as similar *cist* type burials are known from the early medieval period, in Scotland and the north of

England, and these were earlier in date. We thought that this was more likely for a cemetery, right at the gate of a site, known to be one of the principal palace site of the kings of Northumbria in the seventh to ninth centuries.

Bamburgh Research Project investigates

So, the stage was set for the excavation and investigation. It started with a series of three 4m by 2m test pits - two located along the ridge and one sited exactly where the Ordnance Survey said the cemetery was. We pretty much dug the test pit on the 'old' of old Danish burial ground written on the map! Despite its modest size, it's fair to say our trench was well placed, as a full cist burial was revealed within it. It confirmed some of the burials were outlined in stone slabs just as described, but we later found that only a modest percentage of them were. It was an important confirmation, as the site today does not look like it should be a cemetery, though we now know there are reasons for this as the landscape has changed a great deal in the centuries since it was in use. The rediscovery meant we could plan a proper investigation, as we knew where to site a trench to expose burials and evaluate them. The following year we opened up a much larger trench and investigated several of the burials. We still planned this to be a relatively modest investigation, just large enough to help understand if the site really was in danger of erosion, try to develop an idea of its date and learn something about who was buried there.

By the end of 2001 we had the results from a small number of radiocarbon dates and all were of 6th to 7th century AD, leaving us fairly confident that we were investigating an early medieval cemetery and one pre dating the Viking Age. We also now knew that the cemetery contained men, women and children and, thankfully, that there was little sign of the erosion that had been feared from the bone fragment discovery of the 1970s. Given how close the cemetery was to Bamburgh Castle, known to have been a palace of the Northumbrian kings from the early medieval period, and the date of the cemetery, we had the exciting prospect that we might have found burials from the palace of the kings!

Setting the scene for our story

The story of the Bowl Hole cemetery is just a short part of the long history of Northumberland, which has been an occupied landscape for thousands of years, but it is a very fascinating part of that story as it is such a detailed window into the lives of a group of individuals over just a few generations.

The beginning of this story lies back more than 12,000 years ago when the first humans to live in the region arrived after the end of the last Ice Age. They were hunter gathers who followed the herds of animals that they preyed upon. Improving climate allowed temperate plants and animals to venture further and further northwards into an area that only centuries before was Arctic tundra and the humans followed behind to hunt and exploit them into regions like Northern Britain, which before had been under metres of ice. These first inhabitants would have been few in number and consequently have left little trace beyond rare finds of stone tools that preserve very well over many thousands of years. The discovery and excavation of a ring of post-holes cut into the ground that outline a timber house that has been dated back to 7600 BC by radicarbon dating at Howick (about 15km south of Bamburgh) is a rare example of a structure from so early a period. In the main the people of this Mesolithic Age (Middle Stone Age) were frequently on the move following herds of deer, aurochs (extinct large cattle) and even wild boar. They mostly lived in temporary encampments, but some places seem to have been regularly visited, so more permanent structures like the Howick House were rare exceptions.

The Neolithic age introduced farming, and this reached Northumberland in the 4th millennium BC. Sadly, we have little evidence surviving from this time beyond the appearance of new versions of stone tools and some rare communal burial monuments. The main settlements continued to be mostly quite temporary structures that left little trace. It is not until the end of the Neolithic and the early Bronze Age that we start to see monuments more commonly in the landscape. These included stone circles (a fine example of which can be visited at Duddo some 35km to the west of Bamburgh close to the B5364), cairns and burial barrows. Recent genetic studies undertaken across Europe indicates that there was a large influx of people around the Early Bronze Age that substantially replaced the Neolithic population. It is likely that around this time some of the languages that are still spoken in the British Isles today, such as Gaelic and Welsh, first arrived in their original forms.

The Bronze Age (from 2600 BC to around 800 BC) is also when we first start to see the use of metals in society, perhaps unsurprisingly as there is very much a spoiler in the name! At first such exotic materials as bronze and gold was only present in small quantities in the hands of an elite and used for display and showing off, often in an intimidating way when bronze spears and swords are involved. Later when we reach the Iron Age (around 800 BC), metal started to become more common and was even used in everyday items. This was a time of hillforts and warrior elites and it seems that the rock on which Bamburgh Castle stands may have carried just such a fort. We know from archaeological evidence that it was a place where people lived and ate, as the archaeological layers from this time contain animal bone and pottery sherds. Our earliest evidence for occupation is a radiocarbon date from deep in the archaeological layers which shows people were eating meat, and disposing of bones as waste, as early as the tenth century BC. A more recent addition is the exciting discovery of a stone-founded, timber roundhouse of likely Romano-British date (a period often said to be between AD 43 and AD 410, but a little contentious in when it ends). A type of house in use from the Bronze Age to the Roman period. Its presence in the West Ward, far from the summit of the fortress, suggests that numerous such structures stood within the rock fortress. In turn, this implies Bamburgh was a well populated site - from this time to the present day. It is likely to have been a coastal promontory fort - the equivalent of a hill fort. It continued to be occupied during Roman times, but as for most of this period it lay beyond the Roman military frontier. It seems very likely that it would have been the fortress of a tribal leader. Possibly one who was a client of the Roman administration, paid to look out for Roman interests and with access to Roman products, such as the fine Samian pottery whose fragments we find on site along with at least one copper alloy Bow brooch. The more mundane finds such as animal bone can still add to our understanding as they suggest that beef was very popular, as cattle bones considerably outnumbered pig, sheep and goat.

Origins of Northumbria

The end of Roman rule in the region, as with much of Britain, is poorly understood due to a lack of written records. As a consequence, archaeology is not just our best tool for understanding the fifth and sixth centuries, it is often all we have to go on. For the majority of the Roman occupation of Britain, the frontier between the Roman controlled area and the tribal lands lay some 70km to the south of our site, along the line of Hadrian's Wall. Despite this, the Roman influence in the Bamburgh region from the later first century was likely to be substantial. At first this influence was exercised from forts located along Roman Roads north of the wall as far as Tweedmouth and into the Borders Region. Later these forts went out of use, but influence is likely to have remained via client relationships with local chieftains that would have given cooperative chieftains access to prestigious Roman products as described above.

It seems very likely that as the Roman presence diminished that the power-base they offered, through access to treasure or goods, also reduced and this must have led to a change of role for the client chiefs and local military leaders. Perhaps becoming more focussed on military force and control of agricultural resources? It has been suggested, and seems likely, that these successor warlords would have been descended from the last Roman commanders. One clue that this may have been the case is a letter mentioned by Zosimus, a Greek monk and government official from the Eastern Roman Empire, that is said to be from the Emperor Honorius to the cities of Britain. It informed them to look to their own defence as no help from the empire should be expected. One of the few written references we have to this period names a people called the Gododdin and philologists believe this is descended from the tribal name Votadini, known from earlier Roman times as the tribal inhabitants of Northumbria and the eastern Borders. This may indicate a tribal group that might well represent some continuity of settlement and control into the post-Roman period.

Archaeology is in many ways a relatively new discipline and evolved as an academic skill from an amateur tradition in the eighteenth and nineteenth centuries. Antiquarian interests of this time often stemmed from a classical education and focussed on the Roman presence in Britain. The uncovering of stone structures and buildings from the soil soon became a well proven method. A better understanding of the prehistoric and the early medieval periods, where timber structures predominated instead of stone, required substantial advances in archaeological excavation technique that did not take place until after the Second World War. This was the discovery that large open trenches allowed for the subtle soil stains that marked the line of ditches, construction trenches or the rotted remains of timber structures to be traced by eye. After all a building sized rectangular stain in the ground with near right-angled corners is probably not a natural feature! This 'new archaeology' revealed a whole new world of timber architecture. One of the first major excavations of this kind was the uncovering of a timber hall complex at Yeavering in Northumberland by Brian Hope-Taylor, whom we mentioned earlier. He was able to demonstrate that this was an early medieval timber palace site of the Northumbrian kings, mentioned in the pages of Bede - the great eighth century historian from whose writings our understanding of early medieval Britain draws so much.

Conventional history of Bernicia, the northern kingdom of Northumbria as it is named in the few surviving texts of the time, enters history in AD 547 when Ida (the eponymous founder of the dynasty) seized Bamburgh and made it the centre of their new expanding kingdom.

Surprisingly, there is even some poetry, preserved in later Welsh manuscripts, that may, just may, preserve tales of the conflicts fought over control of Northumberland from this time. It even names the *Gododdin*, the tribal group that we mentioned above, as protagonists in one of the battles. This tends to be seen as a part of the conventional story of how the Old-English-speaking Anglo-Saxons arrived in Britain, and those who settled in Northumberland, took control of lands formerly held by the Welsh-speaking British. Ultimately winning out and becoming the kings of Northumbria we hear of in the pages of Bede's history. Archaeologists, looking at the material culture and burial sites, have often questioned this approach, seeing the conventional story as a little too simple. This seems to have been doubly the case for Northumberland, where there has never been much archaeological evidence for the large scale arrival of a new population. And of course the tales of competing dynasties and warlords, stripped down to its core story, is really one of political conflict for power and does not necessarily confirm the older version of events.

Early archaeological work in the region, on the Roman forts along Hadrian's Wall and the forts to the north, had little to say of the end of the Roman presence or the period after. More modern work, using better techniques, has revealed that some of the fort sites - such as Birdoswald in Cumbria - continued to be occupied into the post-Roman period. This would fit in with authority being passed on by the final garrisons and their successors.

There is then an alternate model for the origins of the kingdom of Bernicia, that sees it originating in the Tyne valley, as a successor state to the Roman authority. This may be supported by the name of the kingdom itself as 'Bernicia' translated is something like 'land of the mountain passes'. A fitting title for a kingdom whose origins were around the central wall area, say Corbridge, where roads lead out up through the Cheviots, or down through the Pennines, but not a fitting one for a kingdom centred on the coast around Bamburgh. It might be a case then that the origin myth of 'Ida seizing Bamburgh' lies in an expansion northward of a pre-existing kingdom, which was taking control of territory once controlled by the *Gododdin* tribe. This is a model that also does not see a need for large numbers of Anglo-Saxon warriors arriving in the region and so fits well with the archaeological record.

Bamburgh – the northern capital

We know from archaeological excavation that the fortress of Bamburgh has been an occupied site since the late Bronze Age, but only comes into written history in the middle of the sixth century AD as the principal stronghold of the dynasty that ruled Bernicia - the northern half of the later kingdom of Northumbria. We also know from other, often later, records that Bamburgh originally had the Northern Welsh name '*Din Guardi*'. This led to assumptions that Bamburgh was a fortress taken over by the Bernician dynasty from local Welsh-speaking kings or tribal chiefs. The exciting, recent discovery of a roundhouse in the West Ward provides us with evidence that the site was of regional importance long before the Bernician kings made it their palace. After all, if there is a substantial roundhouse, of likely Roman date, here in the lower-lying, less important part of the fortress, then it seems reasonable that there were many others all the way

The curving section of rubble-stone is part of the foundation of a roundhouse.
A timber wall would have stood on the foundation topped by a thatched roof shaped like a cone. © G. Young

up to the summit of the rock. This is where the hall of a tribal chief would surely have stood. Such a densely settled site was clearly much more important than many of the smaller settlements around it, which would have been little more than family farms. Bamburgh was the equivalent of one of the larger, Iron Age, hill-forts that survived its role through the Roman occupation.

This means when the first 'Anglo-Saxon' kings took Bamburgh as their residence, they were writing a new chapter in a long tradition of great lords ruling the region from the fortress. The first generations of these rulers were not Christians, but according to Bede, worshipped pagan Germanic gods like Woden and Thunor (we know these names today more familiarly as Odin and Thor, their Viking versions). All our evidence from the excavation of the Bowl Hole tells us that it is an early-Christian cemetery site. From history, this would mean that it first came into use from around the early to middle part of the seventh century - at the time of the conversion of Northumbria during the reigns of Edwin (616-632) and Oswald (634-642). Edwin was converted in the 620s after marrying a Christian princess from the Kingdom of Kent, but it is uncertain how much this affected Bamburgh as Edwin (being from the Deiran line, this is the royal family of the southern part of Northumbria who competed with the royals of Bamburgh to control the kingdom) would have drawn his main support from what is now Yorkshire and may have rarely been to Bamburgh. Oswald was from the northern line and Bamburgh must surely have been his principal palace site. After his death, his relics were present in a church within the fortress. This became a centre of religious-cult - venerating him as a saint, and as a result, we can be pretty sure that the cemetery was in use by this time and continued for many generations.

Oswald was described by Bede in glowing terms as a great king, being both a war leader and a pious king who led by example. We know that Bede was writing in part to provide a heroic example for the rulers of his own day, so we can be a little sceptical when we see a king presented to us as such a flawless example of kingship. Despite this, Bede was a good historian and other sources provide support to the idea that Oswald was both important and respected. His reign was short. He was killed in battle in AD 642, but he was not forgotten. His canonisation ensured that he was more renowned in death than in life and even gained a wider European following as a saint.

He was succeeded by his brother Oswui, who ruled until AD 670. Oswui achieved a great feat for an early medieval king of that time - living a long life and dying in his bed. His son Ecgfrith was very much in the warrior tradition, and like his uncle, died in battle. The next king, also a son of Oswui, called Aldfrith, was illegitimate (not the son of Oswui's official wife) and was not expected to rule. As a result, he had an education more suitable for a role in the church, rather than a warrior king. He was more an academic and a diplomat than a warrior and greatly endowed the church. This set Northumbria on route to being an intellectual and cultural powerhouse, rather than a warrior-focussed empire. His rule is viewed as the beginning of the Northumbrian Golden Age, a movement that produced some of the finest works of literary art ever seen in Europe. The greatest example of this is the Lindisfarne Gospels. These were deemed as so perfect by later generations, that they were thought to have been made by angels. It is perhaps this new cultural aspect of Northumbrian life that best explains the varied geographic backgrounds that the scientific analysis of the burials from the cemetery site reveals to us.

Northumbria, in the eighth century, did not again rise to the levels of power over other kingdoms of Britain that it had in the seventh century - when many of its kings were recognised as overlords by other kingdoms. Although it remained an important and independent kingdom, and one with a high degree of intellectual culture within its church. We can see this in the creation of a northern archbishopric at York in AD 735 and also in the presence of Northumbrian scholars, such as Alcuin at the court of Charlemagne the great Frankish king of the eighth century.

Historical records from the ninth century are very rare for Northumbria, which makes it difficult to understand developments. Northumbria did continue as a kingdom and its coinage, which began at the time of Aldfrith (towards the end of the seventh century), continued until at least the middle of the ninth century. York then fell to a Viking army and the kingdom was disrupted. After this time, a Viking kingdom centred in York emerged, and survived until the middle of the tenth century, when England was finally unified under the kings of Wessex (the dynasty of Alfred the Great). To complicate things, the native Northumbrian dynasty also survived and ruled north of the River Tees. Descendants of this line appear at the beginning of the tenth century, as rulers of Bamburgh and allies of the Wessex kings. The Wessex kings, who now styled themselves King of England, never called these northern rulers 'kings', so we see them under titles such as Alderman and Earl. Despite this, their power in the region was undoubted and it lasted until after the Norman Conquest, when the last of them fell in rebellion, and Northumberland finally became just another county of England.

The Bowl Hole Cemetery

The site lies only 300m south-east of the castle. It is on a natural plateau south-west of, and above, a low lying depression in the dunefield - referred to locally as the 'Bowl Hole'. It is this natural feature that gives the cemetery its name. On the west side of the plateau, an area of higher ground extends 450m to the south-east from the base of the castle rock and, as the slope up to it is quite steep, we can be sure that this must mark one side of the cemetery. The southern limit may be defined by a little stream that rises in some wet ground, on the opposite side of the modern road. The plateau itself is 90m north-west to south-east by 40m south-west to north-east.

Today the cemetery lies largely under rough grass, with some encroachment from sycamore and other trees from the wood on the sandstone ridge to its south. There are a number of small sand dunes, up to 10m in diameter and 1m in height. These are likely the remnants of the dunes that kept the site hidden for centuries, before a great storm event caused it to be revealed in the nineteenth century. The soil in the area is composed of sand and silt, but as you dig deeper, you reach a glacial boulder clay - into which many of the graves are deep enough to be cut.

The landscape setting in which we experience the cemetery site today is more than a little different from how it would have appeared when the cemetery was in use. Over the years that we have studied the site, we have gained a substantial amount of evidence of this change. We started by simply looking at the maps for the area, which provided our first clue. From when the 1st Edition of the Ordnance Survey was compiled (around 1860) we can see, that over the following 160 years, a large quantity of dunefield had accumulated. The high tide line of the northern end of the castle had reached all the way to the base of the castle rock and much of the dunefield in the area of the Bowl Hole was absent so has developed since that time. When we investigate the underlying boulder clay and geology, we see that there is nothing to stop the high tide reaching the base of the cemetery plateau, and as the area has clearly been gaining sand for a very long time, this is in fact likely to have been the case. This would also explain why some erosion of the cemetery had occurred in the past. Excavation within the West Ward of the castle would appear to offer some

Part of the burial ground under excavation in 2005. Bamburgh Castle in the background and the high ground that hides the cemetery from the village can be seen to the left on the photo.
© G. Young

evidence to confirm this. Examination of the sides of the deep excavation trenches within the castle reveals that deposits from the medieval period, down to the base of the sequence, shows the soil matrix dominated by silt. Only the most modest sand content, suggesting accumulation is driven by midden-like deposition of food waste by the occupants. This continues to the later medieval period, when sand starts to make up more of the soil layers, and above this we see layers composed of mainly wind-blown sand. This is evidence of the accumulation of dry dunes adjacent to the site at this time, which allowed sand to blow into the site. Prior to the later medieval period, the beach area would have been fully tidal up to the base of the castle rock and without the dry sand that can be easily blown around.

This evidence does suggest that at the time it was in use, the burial ground lay on a distinctive plateau, above a tidal beach with good views out to the north, east and south. Although dominated by the higher sandstone ridge to the west, which would have cut off all views from the site to the landward side. This is significant as St Aidan's church lies in the current village and this must surely be the *vill* (settlement) near Bamburgh where Aidan built a church on land donated by King Oswald, as described by Bede. There would though have been clear views to the palace site on the castle rock from the cemetery at the Bowl Hole, where the church dedicated to St Peter stood in what is now the Inner Ward of the castle. As a result, it is natural to see a connection between the burial ground and this palace church.

The excavated portion of the cemetery at the Bowl Hole was in use for several generations, from at least the early seventh century AD (though some of our radiocarbon dates at least allow for late sixth century) through the eighth century, and perhaps into the ninth century. We have a limited series of radiocarbon dates that form the scientific evidence for the period of time the cemetery was in use, and these are also supported by the few finds that we can date stylistically. These are mostly normal everyday items that a person might be expected to be carrying in life, such as a comb for grooming or a knife and buckle that would have been part of a belt set. The absence of particular type of finds we call 'high status grave goods' (such as weapons and treasure) that were deliberately chosen to accompany the dead is much more to be expected from a cemetery of mostly Christian date. This with the other dating evidence may indicate

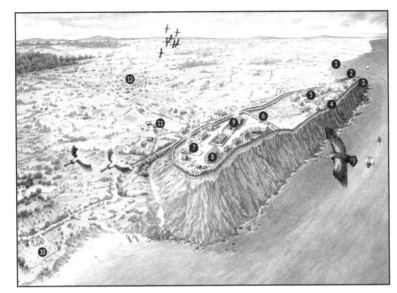

1. Harbour at the shallow inlet

2. St. Oswald's Gate - the Anglo-Saxon entrance to the castle

3. The Gate Hall

4. East Ward

5. West Ward - the industrial heart of the castle complex

6. Box rampart palisade

7. Inner Ward

8. Church

9. The Great Hall

10. Cemetery site

11. Dispersed village

12. Village church complex on the site of the current St Aidan's church

Illustration © Andy Gammon

One of the 'crouched' burials under excavation, showing something of the variety of ways bodies were laid to rest.
© G. Young

that the area of the cemetery we investigated predominantly dated from the AD 620s and later. Even so, it was in use for no short period of time and, throughout that time, many changes would have occurred in Northumbrian society. The burial ground displays a considerable variety in grave orientation, body orientation as well as the presence of a proportion of the graves being outlined in stone. Indeed, it was the fact that a number of the graves were stone-lined (often called a called *cist*) burials that led to the original identification of the burial ground following a storm. Now having explored a more extensive area of the cemetery, we know that only about one-in-five graves have a stone lining - and none of those are fully-outlined all around. It appears therefore that these partial stone linings are only one of the ways that a grave can be marked. Not one of the graves had any indication of a slab at the base or one covering the grave top. Though, in the latter case, some may have been lost through erosion as the original reports from the early nineteenth century do suggest some cases of slab covering.

The majority of the burials were aligned on variations of west-south-west to east-north-east and were quite distinct from the true east to west burials that were concentrated in the southern excavation area explored in 2007. When describing orientation, we first note the end of the grave where the head lies and so it may also be significant that some are oriented the opposite way around (head to the eastern end). A great many of the burials show a degree of flexing, or crouching, where the skeleton lies on its side with the legs drawn up. This can vary from very modest bending of the knees, to the legs being tucked up in an almost foetal position. Crouching is very common in the cemetery, and present to a degree across full the extent of it. This suggests it was done for a significant reason and meant something in the burial process for the individual or those burying them. In one instance, it is even present in the southernmost investigated part of the cemetery to the south an area we think were the used later in the life of the cemetery. A surprising number of bodies are laid in their graves face down. This is called a 'prone burial'. Such burials do occur in cemeteries of the medieval period, but the Bowl Hole stands out in the sheer number of them, which must be of significance and we will consider what this may mean later.

Given the size of the cemetery and the variations within it - and its being in use for several generations - it is important to try and work out how the cemetery was used and expanded, so we can see trends over time. A good starting point for this is to look at where the original burials are likely to have been. It seems reasonable to assume that earlier burials would be concentrated on the plateau area closer to the palace and later burials further away when the prime positions were filled up. As the true east-to-west burials lay well to the south, that seems to suggest that these are a later phase within the cemetery when this conventional 'Christian' orientation became more commonplace. In addition, although care clearly was taken to avoid disturbing previous burials, there are some instances of one graving cutting into another and this gives us a definite order of burial in a small number of cases. One further property of the burials that is seen as an indicator of date is the variation in depth of burial. There are a group of burials in the main excavation area, which is closer to the castle, that are very shallow. In some cases, so much so that they lie immediately below the turf horizon. These graves must have originally been dug to a sensible depth. That means a significant erosion event must have occurred during the life of the cemetery and the burials that are deeper were dug after this event. Given the circumstances that led to the rediscovery of the cemetery following a storm-erosion event, this seems the likely mechanism for such erosion in the more distant past. The main collection of these super shallow burials, some so eroded that they are merely collections of bones, are on the seaward side of the main dig area - but not quite the closest to the castle. This may mean that some of the earliest burials have been entirely lost!

A series of quite shallow burials - but the earliest that are complete - lie at the north end of the cemetery and are generally the closest to the palace. Some are within crude pit-like graves and either in a crouched position, on their sides, or a little too disturbed to tell. The rest are laid out full-length. All are from northern Britain or the west of Ireland. Significantly these areas can be associated with Oswald in exile and as a new ruler establishing his place as king.

The next group are deeper and are generally arranged in rows, in two groups, with something of a gap between them as if they were avoiding the central part of the site. The group contained a mix of ages, both males and females and are also quite varied in the way that they are arranged in the grave - being a mix of crouched burials and those on their back, but also with two who were face down. The next group identified lay to the south-west of this one and contained a high proportion of crouched burials, seven compared to five, on their backs and also with two face down. Other than this, they are similar to the previous group and perhaps represent more of a subgroup with little real change of burial practice.

This brings us to two further groups one the extreme east side of the area and the other are on a similar alignment to the west of the previous group. They are distinctive in being much closer to true east-to-west burials, with most just slightly oriented with the west end of the grave a little to the south. They are rather spread out and not in rows, which could be the result of the area beginning to fill up, with burials added where the gaps remained.

To the south and west of the excavated area we can see a further group of burials that lie close together in the south-west part of the cemetery and are as with some of the earlier groups oriented more south-west to north-east than true east-to-west burials. It would be tempting to see these as part of the earlier groups that were similarly oriented, and they did also contain a pretty even mixture of full-length burials (on their backs) and crouched burials and must have been buried in two phases, as there was intercutting of graves between them. This group being located in an area distinctly further from the palace and further to the south might make them a distinct later group, but we should not rule out that they could match the others on a similar orientation and represent a deliberately separate burial zone.

The final phase of burials in the main excavation area are eleven truly east-to-west burials. They are clustered in a group in a north-to-south line and are unusual as six of them are buried face down, which makes this the only grouping where this burial style is predominant in the whole cemetery. It seems likely that this is significant, and we will see when we discuss the isotope data (that can give us an insight into where people grew up) that, excitingly, this is indeed the case.

Finally, we come to a smaller excavation area that lies some 30m to the south-east of the main trench. This trench was investigated in 2007, our last season at the site. It was placed here to give a little insight into how the cemetery may have changed as it spread away from the palace. We assumed that this area was in use later than the main excavation area closer to the palace and the radiocarbon dates that we have bear this out as they are concentrated in the eighth century AD and perhaps remaining in use in the ninth century. The earliest burials in this area are two, rather disturbed, crouched burials that are followed by ten later east-to-west burials, which are in four lines across the excavation area. All are arranged almost full-length, with only one mildly crouched, with the head to the west-side. They are close to true east-to-west orientation. Compared to the other excavation area it lacks the variation of orientation and looks very much like a conventional, later-medieval cemetery. This may be because it is a little later in date and by this time, we are seeing that the style of how someone is buried has begun to become quite standard for a Christian community.

Who was buried in the Bowl Hole?

We are so fortunate in the cemetery that the bone preservation of the 98 discrete individuals identified (we have evidence from bone fragments of a somewhat larger population), due to the sandy soil, is really very good. This means that it is possible for someone with medical knowledge to measure stature and, in most adults, determine if they were male or female. This means we know that the population was fairly evenly mixed with 45% male and 42% female - with 13% not able to be determined. We also see ages ranging from newborn to elderly - with 31% non-adults. These numbers show that we have family groups represented, making the palace population a community and not a male-dominated garrison.

We can determine the age of a skeleton quite accurately - up to the age of 26 - by mapping out what bones have fused during growth. Older adults are much harder to age, but it is possible to make an educated guess if there are signs that they have lived a long life. In addition, muscle attachment points on the bone will often tell us if the person had a very active life. There can also be indications of repetitive activities from marks left on teeth or bone. It is not usually easy to be sure how someone dies, but some diseases and accidents do leave marks or scars on the bone and so we can often tell something about how healthy someone was during life.

Palace society

Bamburgh, being one of the Northumbrian palace sites, was a place for royalty and the high echelons of society, and so, these are at least some of the people we should expect to be represented within the cemetery. So, if we want to understand who our Bowl Hole population were, we need to know who would live in, or visit, a palace and cult-centre like Bamburgh within this time period.

Kings originate from tribal leaders, and although they had a religious role - perhaps even more so before Christianity - they were first and foremost war leaders. It is thought that kingdoms in England formed from tribal groups in the 6th century AD. There were royal dynasties, and an illustrious royal pedigree was certainly seen as an advantageous thing, but there was no orderly succession from father to eldest son - as seen in the late-middle ages. It was in fact fairly common for brothers to succeed each other as young or inexperienced children, who lacked experience or a formidable reputation in battle, would not be seen as able to protect or expand the kingdom. In practice, a royal dynasty was a pool of potential male heirs from which a new king would be selected.

The next tier of society were the aristocratic warriors who formed the royal army. They would be given arms and armour by the king, when they swore to serve him till death, and would hope by doing good service at court and at war (as young men) to be given a lifetime grant of land to farm - and bring up a family - later in life. At the time when the Bowl Hole came into use as a cemetery, such granted land was not passed down to their descendants but went back to the crown at death, so their sons would then have to go through the process of earning a grant again. This started to change during the lifetime of the cemetery as new forms of land tenure, introduced at first for land endowments to the church, became more common in wider society.

Kings at this early time did not rule from a fixed capital but moved around their lands, from royal estate to royal estate, consuming the rents due to them in the form of food, mead and beer - feeding their accompanying entourage in the process. This frequent movement occurred not just to use up the food-tax in the most efficient manner, as it is easier to move people than heavy supplies, but also had the benefit of allowing the king to be seen and to enact justice. Both of these were important at a time when government was a very personal thing. Bamburgh was therefore one of many royal estates, although we know from the historical records that some such estates were more important than others. We can tell this because they are places where the important festivals, such as Christmas and Easter, were celebrated or because they appear again and again in the records. Bamburgh was foremost among these in Northumbria.

We should imagine Bamburgh being visited by a throng of folks when the court was present. They would feast and participate in the theatre of government, and of course, in some cases, also fall ill, die and end up being buried in the Bowl Hole. Our evidence that the cemetery contained a balance of sexes and ages tells us that the court was comprised of families and was not at all just a male-dominated war band.

As Christianity became the religion of the Northumbrian kingdom, churchmen would have been ever present at court and part of the life of government. Not the least because for much of the medieval period they were the only literate people able to make records, write diplomatic letters to fellow kings and to read those sent in return.

In the absence of the court, Bamburgh would have been a much less crowded place but never one lacking a population. We can expect a reeve (an aristocratic royal official) to have been the king's representative in his absence, running the palace and the estate lands around it. Servants and the crafts people - needed to keep the structures in good order - would have been present and also those who organised the farm rents and maintained the stores. There is another group we know, from the archaeological record, to have been at Bamburgh. In what is now the 'West Ward', we have evidence of metalworking being undertaken on a substantial scale. Large quantities of a waste product called 'hammer scale' (produced when smithing iron) together with numerous copper alloy materials - and even small quantities of gold - make us think that craftspeople producing arms and armour were based here as a permanent production centre. It seems likely that some, or all of them - together with their families - would have been buried in the Bowl Hole along with the courtiers. One last group we might expect are pilgrims visiting the relics of St Oswald. We know from historical records that pilgrimage was common and encouraged, at least amongst the classes of society that had the resources to travel and who were pious. In fact, it seems very logical that such pilgrimages may well have been more common later in life when ensuring your place in heaven may have been a little more on the mind. As a result, it is quite possible that elderly or ill pilgrims could have contributed substantially to the cemetery population.

Archaeological evidence for the palace at Bamburgh

The stature and health evidence from the cemetery population strongly suggests that they were high status individuals, given relatively little evidence for malnutrition or the diseases of poverty compared to most early medieval cemetery populations. One health issue did really stand out though and that was the terrible incidence of tooth decay and the number of abscesses suggesting terrible dental hygiene, which can be seen as an indicator of excessive consumption and a high status indicator. The result of this evidence, combined with the close physical relationship with the fortress palace site, means that we have good reason to see the Bowl Hole as the cemetery for the royal palace population and associate it with the church - present within the Inner Ward - that held the relics of St Oswald. Had there been any doubt about this, then surely the extraordinary variation in the childhood origins of the individuals (shown by the scientific analysis of isotopes recovered from the teeth) would leave no further doubt that we are seeing a cross section of the high status mobile top layer of society and not a local farming population.

Palace of the kings

We have seen that Bamburgh was an important fortress from prehistoric times and, around the middle of the sixth century AD, became the palace fortress of the royal dynasty that ruled the northern kingdom of *Bernicia* and then later the wider kingdom of Northumbria. The earliest named king was called Ida and he is seen generally to have been the founder of the dynasty. He, as with many of his successors, is really just a name in a dynastic list. It is not until the later part of that century that we find a history that can flesh out a little more about a king and his reign. King Aethelfrith ruled *Bernicia* from AD 593 and was the first king to unite the two kingdoms of *Bernicia* and *Deira* that combined to form Northumbria. The little evidence we have for the early years of this dynasty associates it very closely with Bamburgh and it is easy to imagine the formidable fortress being a safe haven for a warrior dynasty, struggling to establish its power base in the region. Bede tells us that Aethelfrith was hugely successful in conquering territory, expanding his kingdom and that he ruled up to AD 616, but that his reign - as was so often the case in this period - ended in death and defeat on the battlefield. Power was a very personal thing at that time and the authority rested with a king and his reputation - and the warband that such reputation would attract. There were no standing armies and few enduring institutions within an early medieval kingdom, so power ebbed and flowed with the fortunes of the dynasty.

Aethelfrith's death was linked to dynastic rivalry and his attempt to force a rival king to kill their heir of a competing Northumbrian royal dynasty. This was Edwin, of the *Deiran* royal house, the southern of the two former kingdoms that had come together to form Northumbria. And it was Edwin who gained from his fall, becoming king and driving Aethelfrith's sons into exile. Edwin, who appears from the page of Bede, as a proud and ambitious man was eager to further raise the power and profile of Northumbria and, to support this, he arranged a marriage to the Kentish Royal House. The Kingdom of Kent had converted to Christianity a generation earlier and one of the stipulations for the marriage was that Princess Aethelburh be allowed to continue as a Christian. In addition Edwin promised to convert and allow the preaching of Christianity to his subjects. He appears to have dithered a little about this but his surviving an assassination attempt, and the success of a subsequent war, seems to have confirmed to him that Christianity was the way to go. Bede tells us that a priest called Paulinus, travelling with the royal court, carried out mass baptisms - including one at the palace site at Yeavering, not far from Bamburgh. It is therefore from the time of Edwin's conversion in AD 627 that we see Northumbria as a Christian kingdom and this is perhaps our best guess for the early use of the Bowl Hole cemetery.

As was so often the case at in the seventh century, Edwin too died in battle, defeated by an alliance of the kings of Gwynedd (in Wales) and Mercia (Midlands England). This resulted in a period of instability as Northumbria was partially occupied. It was seen as an opportunity by Aethelfrith's sons to regain the crown and so the eldest Eanfrith tried and failed to retake the kingdom, lasting in power for only a matter of months. The next eldest, Oswald, was more successful. He won a desperate battle against Cadwallon, king of Gwynedd and became king. It is significant for our story that Oswald was a committed Christian, having been converted to Christianity in exile, and had close ties to the monastery of Iona. The conversion under

Edwin was in part a political event, but Oswald was genuinely devout. His reign consolidated Christianity in Northumbria - it saw the founding of monasteries and the endowment of land to the church. This included Lindisfarne, the island monastery seen across the water from the palace of Bamburgh. His devotion was significant for Bamburgh as well, as his canonisation after his death at the hands of Penda - the pagan king of Mercia - resulted in Bamburgh becoming a royal cult centre, and a focus of pilgrimage, in addition to being a palace site.

Oswald's brother Oswui (pronounced Os-wee) succeeded him and was also a very successful ruler. For much of the seventh century, Northumbria was the most powerful Kingdom in England and was of significance beyond its borders. Later kings did not enjoy as much power or fame but Northumbria remained an important, if no longer pre-eminent, kingdom. Church-life was another story, with Northumbrian monasticism and scholarship gaining an international reputation and developing contacts across the continent.

What a visit to the fortress would have been like

Even today Bamburgh, a castle perched on a rock outcrop by the sea, in a still rural part of the English countryside, is a striking place to visit. In an ancient land with so much preserved heritage, it still stands out. Now imagine living in a society where almost all buildings are made of timber and are a single storey. Tall buildings, or even the grand cathedrals of the later middle ages, are unknown. At such a time, a fortress on its rock towering over the landscape would have struck those seeing it for the first time with genuine awe. Nature has quite fashioned it in such a way, and at earlier times when there was a much reduced dunefield, and the high tide of the North Sea washed up to the base of the rock, it was even more spectacular and special than today.

The Bowl Hole cemetery was an important place for the inhabitants of Bamburgh and those visiting the palace, but it was a rather secluded place. Shielded from the landward side by high ground, it looked out to

sea at the wider world and back towards the dominating palace fortress to its north. The defended palace was deliberately sited to be the standout landmark, with its tall buildings high on its rock outcrop and visible for many kilometres around. The largest of these structures would have been the great hall and the church, which was the focus of the important cult centre for St Oswald. These would have been lofty gabled and decorated with primary colours and perhaps even shining gold in places, displaying its importance and the wealth of its royal patrons for all to see. Built, sited and decorated quite literally to inspire awe in any beholder.

The landscape around would have been very agricultural, and so not all that different to that of today. With fields under plough and pasture and smoke rising from isolated, farming settlements scattered every few kilometres around the area. Bamburgh would also have had a village and church close to the palace, almost certainly where the current village stands. Village buildings would have been built of timber throughout, as would the church on the site of the modern Saint Aidan's - where you can view the ossuary today.

At its highest point, the bedrock beneath the castle rises 45m above sea level. It is rather uneven, rising and falling over its plateau, descending to 30m above sea level at its lowest point at the northern end. It was an elongated north-to-south outcrop that is 300m long and varies from 70m wide down to 15m and is 3.3 hectares in area.

We are very fortunate that at a time from which few written records survive, there is a brief description of what Bamburgh was like in AD 774. This is courtesy of a scribal digression when recording that a king had been driven into exile and had fled first to Bamburgh. It is only a paragraph, but still very informative, telling us that the City of Bebba (a translation of Old English *Bebbanburh* - what Bamburgh was called at that time) is extremely well fortified with a hollowed entrance ascended by steps. This part of the text is almost certainly describing St Oswald's Gate at the northern end of the castle, where the rock reaches its lowest point (compared to land around) and where steps extend down from the interior within a natural cleft in the bedrock. The text then tells us that a church, of "beautiful architecture", stands on the summit of the hill and contains the preserved arm of St Oswald as a relic. To the west (and at the highest point) is a well, excavated by "extraordinary labour". And extraordinary the labour of its cutting must have been, as it is 45m deep and cut through bedrock throughout!

At the time that the Bowl Hole cemetery was first in use, Bamburgh was a timber fortress containing timber buildings. The skills for quarrying and building in stone had been forgotten as the influence of, and connections to, Rome ended. As a timber fort it was vulnerable to fire, though the palisade that would have defended the summit from attack was just the last defensive contribution built by humans. Much of the work had been done by nature, millions of years ago, when magma, from a long extinct volcano, set as a rock called dolerite underground. This rock was so hard that as the sedimentary rock around it was eroded away, it remained and stood out as a dark and menacing natural fortress in the landscape.

Had we been able to visit in the early seventh century, we would have approached over land from the area of the modern village (where an earlier version of a settlement would have stood even then) towards the cleft of St Oswald's Gate, the main entrance to the palace fortress that lay at the north-end as the rock plateau within a narrow cleft in the rock. It is reached today via a curved path that rises up in steps to the gate within the cleft. It would have looked a little different at the time of our cemetery as it is unlikely the outworks that we see today, which are medieval and post medieval in date, would have been present, though the steps or equivalent likely were. Also, the ivy that we see climbing and covering the rock face is a relatively modern arrival, as photos from as recently as the sixties and seventies show very little of it. One big difference back then compared to today, would be for anyone approaching the palace from the sea. Whilst similar from a distance, up close the beach has changed a great deal. This is because the dune field with the Marram grass, which is now very substantial, was not present back then. The tidal beach reached up to the base of the rock and we have good reason to think a small port was present, within a modest inlet, right next to the gate but now cut off from the sea. In a time when travel by sea, at least in summer, was easier and more practical that by land over poor roads, this may well have been the place of arrival of many, even the majority, of visitors to the palace.

Whether you arrived by land or sea, the narrow, climbing entrance was your way in and access would certainly have been controlled and the way guarded. Climbing the steps up to a wooden gate - over which the timber wall would have spanned like a bridge - you would have been questioned by armed warriors and your intentions and reason for your visit would have needed approval. We have previously described how a hall stood atop the gate cleft on your left as you climbed, perhaps casting a deep shadow and looking quite intimidating. This would have been after you passed through the defended perimeter, with its timber - and likely later stone - wall and through what I am sure would have been a very solid timber gate, decorated with elaborate iron fittings intended to impress.

Detail from Reconstruction Illustration
© Andy Gammon

Archaeological investigation by the Bamburgh Research Project has indeed revealed evidence for a timber wall close by the gate. At first it was a palisade set in post-holes, cut into the bedrock, but this was then replaced by a stone rubble foundation on which a timber structure would have been built. It is likely this later stage of the timber fortress wall was a box rampart (two walls connected together with a wall walk and timber extending up on the outside high enough to provide cover to the defenders), a little like a long, snaking, very narrow building wrapped around the edge of the rock. The archaeological excavations in this area also provides evidence for buildings inside the defences. A large timber hall, 12m by 7m, stood immediately above the gate cleft, just inside the wall, and must have dominated the entranceway at that time. In fact, as it was large and very well made, we assume that this may have been the hall occupied by a royal official who controlled access to the palace.

The West Ward from the air showing Trench 3 to the left of the windmill and Trench 1 to the right. St Oswald's Gate is seen descending through the wall in its rock cleft and the low lying ground beyond the gate to the right may have been a port now cut off from the sea and silted up.
© G. Young

A visitor aiming to be received at court would have continued along a road around the natural mound, where the disused windmill built in 1800 now stands. This was the site of a tower in the later medieval period and it is possible that towers were also present along the perimeter defences at this earlier time. Sadly, we just don't have the evidence for them at Bamburgh but a stone tower, called the Anglian Tower (that you can visit today in the museum gardens at York) is almost certainly from the right period, so they did exist at that time. Excavation conducted by the Bamburgh Research Project, within the West Ward (that the road passed through on the way) has revealed a busy industrial zone. One of the most striking discoveries within the excavation of this area (BRP Trench 3) was a substantial cobbled, yard surface from precisely the time of the Bowl Hole cemetery, as it was dated to the seventh to eighth centuries. We have interpreted this as a deliberate, planned, construction of an industrial area, with timber buildings constructed around a yard surface that leads off westwards from the road up to the heart of the fortress. A stone-lined water channel and a series of hearths suggests smithing was undertaken here. We also have a considerable body of metal objects that attest to the type of materials being made, repaired or recycled here. The most dramatic finds are the two pattern-welded swords that were found by Hope-Taylor, right next to Trench 3, when excavating his first trench within Bamburgh Castle in 1960. These are from our era but may have been deposited a little later after the cemetery went out of use (or its area of interment moved further to the south). Finds from within the BRP excavation trench are a little less exciting, but

The best preserved of the two early medieval swords found in the West Ward. A clear reflection of the warrior society of the royal court.
© G. Young

43

still include items such as a shield boss and a pattern-welded, fighting knife, called a *seax*, as well as some fragments of unlinked chain mail, lost during the manufacturing process.

The road from the entrance would then have led further up hill to the Inner Ward, passing through the East Ward along the way. This area of the castle is rather uneven, with some steep slopes, and so is unlikely to have contained many substantial buildings. We have to speculate on what else we might see on the way to the summit of the hill and the great hall. Granaries and other food storage buildings would have been present somewhere within the fortress, along with some accommodation buildings. Perhaps elsewhere than Trench 3 in the West Ward or present on some of the flatter parts of the East Ward. More speculative is the possible presence of stables for royal horses, as such animals were a status symbol as well as an important means of transport. Other animals lived within the fortress as we see them represented as bones in the archaeological record. These included dogs and cats.

The Inner Ward, at the summit of the hill, is a relatively flat area quite suitable for building. It would have been the heart of the fortress, then as now. The most important buildings of the royal place, like the church and the great hall, would have stood here. It is the most prominent and visible part of the fortress with an open view of the landscape, and therefore is the prime site for important buildings intended to display power or prestige. To be seen, and to see out from. As it was the focus of the important buildings, from the distant past right up to the present day, the opportunity to undertake archaeological excavation has been a rare event. This means that the few occasions when it was possible are important and the results fascinating, despite their modest scale. Sadly, excavation through the large lawn at the centre of the inner ward - which was undertaken as part of the Channel Four 'Time Team' Episode - showed that the area had been badly disturbed by later activity, particularly it seems in the nineteenth century, so little in the way of evidence for early activity survives. A couple of rock cut features at the very base of that trench may indicate some structural evidence does survive, if on a rather small scale. Excavation in and around the ruins of the twelfth century chapel, at the south end of the ward, has been much more successful as the presence of the medieval chapel helped preserve the area - discouraging other building.

Trenches here revealed up to 2m depth of early layers beneath the modern ground surface.

By looking at the evidence of a series of smaller trenches, and plotting down the results on a plan, we can build up a picture of the area. The most exciting discovery from this is the presence of a substantial, mortar-bonded stone building, beneath the medieval church. It is on a slightly different alignment, not being true east to west but more west-north-west to east-south-east, with corners poking out of the north and south walls of the medieval chapel. As it lies beneath the later church it must be earlier, and this is really interesting given the church was built in the later twelfth century. As the earlier building was built in stone it must have been of some importance and likely lasted a good while before being knocked down and replaced, so there is a decent chance that it might even date back to the time our cemetery was in use! We can't know if this is a part of the church, mentioned by Bede, that contained the relics of St Oswald and which we think is closely linked to the cemetery, but it is at least a possibility which is very exciting indeed.

Whether this building was the church or just a nearby building, we know from written history that the church was present from the mid seventh century and so the first version must have been built of timber. As stone construction became possible from the later part of the seventh century, it is very likely that the church - being such an important building - would be one of the first structures replaced in stone. Perhaps this is inferred by the description we quoted from AD 774 that described it as of "beautiful architecture". This shrine to St Oswald, which would have been its great treasure and the focus of the attention of pilgrims from the mid seventh century. Saints were seen as intermediaries to heaven, so gifts and veneration was a direct line to divinity. A seventh century crypt, which once contained relics of St Wilfred, still survives beneath Hexham Abbey. Its access ways were carefully constructed to channel and control pilgrims visiting the shrine. This gives us some insight into what must have been present at Bamburgh at that time. Although we have good reason to think there was no underground crypt on the summit of the castle rock, and the church would have surely been smaller, the desire to hold the relic securely - and control how pilgrims approached and viewed it - was likely common to both. This sacred place must be one of the prime reasons that such a varied and far travelled group of individuals was found within the cemetery, perhaps even greater in its attractive qualities compared to the royal palace, which only held the full court as certain select times of year.

Also in the Inner Ward, in addition to the church, we can assume that a great hall would have been present where the king held court. Feasts and important ceremonies would have been held here and the building, because of its status, would have been lavishly decorated, painted, carved and adorned with tapestries - and perhaps even in some areas with gold leaf, the product of some of the best craftsmen of that age. Just like the church, this would originally have been a timber building - rebuilt later in stone.

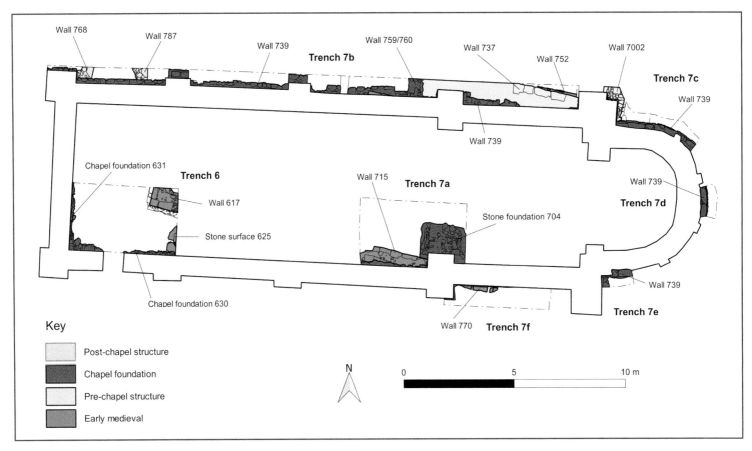

Archaeological investigations around the modern chapel have revealed the medieval foundations and early medieval wall lines that could be associated with a later stone church!

Even though great events in the royal hall would have been spread out over the year, their scale and drama would have been immense. A royal court feasting at Christmas or Easter would have been raucous and impressive. A packed hall, food and drink aplenty, and much noise from laughter, chat and music. Ritual and entertainment. The epic poem Beowulf, perhaps first composed in the form we know in Northumbria, could have been recited by a bard in just such a hall. Also, the sworn dedication of the young, high status men - who composed the royal army in war - would have taken place in the hall in front of an audience. They would have been given gifts of armour and weapons by the king and in turn would have sworn loyalty to death. Written evidence, such as Beowulf, tells us that this gift was bestowed from the royal chair called the 'giftstool' and was undertaken in a formal ceremony in the great feasting hall. This chair would have been on a raised platform or at least in a prominent position and was effectively the king's throne. Extraordinarily, we may have a fragment of one surviving at Bamburgh today. Found buried in the grounds in the nineteenth century, thought at first to be a fragment of a decorated stone cross, this carved stone fragment was finally identified as part of the arm of a stone chair by Professor Rosemary Cramp - as recently as the 1980s. The style of its carved decoration suggests a date in the eighth century, so it would have been in use only in the later phases of the cemetery site. Perhaps like the hall, church and defences, a later stone replacement for a timber original? It is amazing though that we can still look on part of a royal throne from more than 1000 years ago. It provides us with a direct, physical link between our times and those of our cemetery inhabitants. There is a good chance that many looked on this throne and may even have seen one of the Northumbrian kings sit upon it.

One final small archaeological trench, just to the outside of the medieval church, was particularly fascinating despite its size and awkward positioning. A wall had been identified just beneath the turf of a flower border, by the castle groundsman during the summer of 2007. Investigation showed this to be of Norman date and, furthermore, a continuation of the Inner Ward perimeter wall. This must have been the original line of the wall, before it was altered by a kink introduced to increase the area of the inner Ward and allow for a larger church to be built in the twelfth century. Excitingly, this wall stood on another earlier, cruder, stone wall that must surely be early medieval in date. This tells us that the timber fortress, we described earlier, was also rebuilt in stone just like some of the important buildings. A stone fortress with stone buildings within it, set on the dramatic rock outcrop in a landscape otherwise populated by small timber houses, must have been a dramatic site indeed in its day. Stunning and intimidating when seen for the first time.

The cult of St Oswald

Aelred, Abbot of Rievaulx - a twelfth century church chronicler - related a story of the return of St Oswald's head from Bamburgh to Lindisfarne, sometime after its removal from the monastery. His head (along with his arms and hands) had been recovered from stakes on the battlefield where he died in AD 642, by his brother Oswiu, having been displayed as trophies after his death. These had become important relics after his canonisation as a saint. It seems that the head may have been taken to Bamburgh by King Eadberht (ruled AD 737 to 758) when he forcibly took Bishop Cynewulf from the church at Lindisfarne. This was after Cynewulf's granted sanctuary to Offa, son of Aldfrith, who had rebelled against Eadberht. Aelred tells the story of its recovery back to Lindisfarne in some detail, describing how a pious, old man had a vision of St Cuthbert, who instructed him to recover the head for the Lindisfarne community. The account describes how he is said to have done this after attending mass in the church. He left the church towards a nearby cemetery, where his horse was tied, but deliberately left his gloves in the church as a pretext to return there alone. Having pulled off his ruse, he rode off and the theft was not discovered until the next day. It is a quaint little tale of little interest to historians but takes on a greater significance when we are considering the Bowl Hole cemetery and its relation to the palace site. There is a steep stair, that exits the Inner Ward from a point next to the medieval church, which descends through a tunnel vault through the Inner Ward wall, down to the twelfth century Great Gate. Outside the story related by Aelred, we have no reason to assume that this entrance and route predated the construction of this later gate. This narrative which links the church to the area of the cemetery, through a much shorter route than down through the fortress and out through St Oswald's Gate, would certainly have been a more convenient way to reach the cemetery site had it existed as described.

Food and diet

The soil conditions within Bamburgh castle, with its high levels of wind-blown beach sand like the cemetery, provide conditions that are very good for preservation of animal bone. The main focus for archaeological excavation has been within the West Ward at the northern extent of the castle, but as we have seen, there has been some limited excavation within the Inner Ward as well.

Although the evidence recovered from the Inner Ward is much more limited that the West Ward, it still shows important variations that inform us about how processing and consumption of meat varied within the palace site. The animal bone in the West Ward shows 45% cattle, 34% sheep/goat and 9% pig, with small quantities of horse and domestic fowl. The Inner Ward shows 65% cattle, 19% sheep/goat and 4% pig. Cattle it seems is particularly prominent in the Inner Ward assemblage and this seems to be consistent between the Romano-British and early medieval periods. One other aspect that shows difference is that the Inner Ward bone shows a general lack of head and hoof parts, compared to the West Ward where these are very well represented. This suggests that cattle are entering the palace complex on the hoof, but that the better meat cuts are consumed in the Inner Ward after butchering. Entirely consistent of course with the high status role of the Inner Ward at the heart of the palace. If we needed any further proof of this then the presence of wild fowl and even a crane bone, indicating hunting for the table, was also present in the Inner Ward.

The dominance of cattle bone would be consistent with the status of the palace site in the period, but also perhaps shows that royal tribute (kind of military tax) and food rents would often be moved around as cattle on the hoof. Wealth at such an early time was often expressed in the possession of cattle.

An initial crude assessment of the collected bone suggested very low quantities of fish were present in the early medieval period, but now a somewhat more detailed analysis seems to suggest that this may only be true of Trench 3 (industrial area) and not of Trench 1 (gate complex). This may suggest a status difference reflected in food consumption and disposal between the site areas. Something we might have suspected given we think that an important official lodged at the gate to control access.

What did they wear?

Female dress in the fifth to sixth centuries consisted of a sleeveless dress over a sleeved undergarment and was held in place by two brooches near the collar bones. It is in fact the presence of these metal brooches found in graves with skeletons that provides much of our evidence for clothing in the earliest periods. In the seventh century new fashions from Europe reached England, along with Christianity, and with this we see the replacement of the double brooches with a single one as the dress was now often a single garment. Head coverings were very common from this time, staying in fashion right up to the twentieth century, and with the introduction of Christianity, even veils were increasingly a part of female dress. Male dress was a little more simple in the main and consisted of a tunic, probably no more than knee length, with trousers. Wool was the most common material for clothes, but linen was also available, although rarer, and was often used for underclothes - being softer on the skin than wool. High status individuals would have access to finer cloth and rare, possibly imported, dyes to create brighter colours. Their clothing would have been less practical (and less easy to keep clean) and more a statement of wealth and rank. They would have adorned their garments with embroidery and other time-consuming, and therefore expensive, trimmings and embellishments to make their garments look more impressive. Embroidery was one of the activities that high status women would undertake. In fact, pre-Norman Conquest England was famous in Europe for the impressive quality of its embroidery. One of the indicators we have for lifetime activity from the skeletal remains, is the presence of wear patterns on the front teeth of some of the women that suggest repeated gripping of thread in the mouth, quite in line with them undertaking embroidery. With higher status individuals, it was likely leather and fur was also worn, and in some instances perhaps, even silk - which would have been imported from Asia. Colour came from natural materials of course but some, such as purple, could be very expensive and rare.

Shoes were worn by both sexes and would have been of leather. Cloaks were a frequent additional covering for outdoor wear and were very effective in protecting an individual from the often cold climate. Belts were common and often had some basic accessories such as a pouch and knife. The iron buckle that would fasten the belt and the blade of the knife are not uncommon items found in the cemetery as they will survive for centuries, unlike leather or cloth.

A royal palace of course is intended to host the royal court and many of those attending would be drawn from the aristocratic warrior class. As such, arms and armour were a specialist kind of clothing and possession that would have been seen at court. Indeed, we have good archaeological evidence from the West Ward that the manufacturing of this specialised equipment was undertaken on site.

Most are familiar with the images of early medieval warriors on the Bayeux Tapestry, and whilst some two to three hundred years later than our time, it is not too far from the warriors of that earlier age. Metal armour in the form of mail (interlocking rings or iron) would defend the torso and upper arms - down to the elbow - and would reach down to the waist or upper legs. It's a matter of some academic discussion how common helmets were. The Bayeux Tapestry shows many conical shaped helmets with nose guards, but the more elaborate and complex types of helmet - such as the impressive one discovered within the Sutton Hoo ship burial - represent such a lavish investment of skill and labour that they cannot have been commonplace. Whilst it is very likely that such complex helmets - which cover the head, face and neck with plate and mail - are likely to be the highest of status symbols and quite rare, the vulnerability of the head in battle must surely mean that simpler head protection was a lot more common that often thought. Spears would have been the main weapon, carried with swords and perhaps the occasional axe, and round, wooden shields with a central, metal cover for the hand grip as the main type of defence.

Courtly warriors were drawn from the highest status and richest people in society, and additionally weapons and armour was often the gift of the king, so we can be sure that the lavish decoration seen on helmets, sword hilts and shields - which might include dragons and fierce birds, depicted in metal alloy and often even gold plate - were common decorations. Such weapons were as much for show as for use, after all. That said we even have tragic evidence of just how deadly they could be from one of our skeletons in the cemetery. The young man with an extreme weapon injury all down one side of his body is a sad, but dramatic, evidence of this.

The people of the Bowl Hole

The extraordinary insight that the scientific examination has given us into the origins of the cemetery population was, without a doubt, the most unexpected and fascinating result from the excavation. The widely varied population, which shows just how important Bamburgh was at this time, must be based on the double draw of being both a royal palace and a cult centre for an important saint. Oswald was very well known in later medieval Europe, much more so than today, and had a number of cult centres in northern continental Europe.

It seems that very few burials are of people who grew up in or around Bamburgh and north Northumberland, one very good reason to associate the cemetery to the palace and not the wider community farming in the landscape. The Northumbrian court would have drawn its members from wider Northumbria, though it is suspicious that Yorkshire - the heart of the southern half of Northumbria - is very poorly represented. This causes us to speculate that perhaps there were two royal circuits that the king would have attended over the year. However, those who sent representation to palace sites in the south, did not do so in the north and vice versa. In addition to Northumbrian nobles, those of other kingdoms are likely to have been present as exiles or hostages. Remember Oswald, his brothers and their families were in exile for a decade and a half before they successfully regained the throne. It is appropriate then that the area of Argyll is represented. One such burial - an older male who died in around the mid to late seventh century - was born in the general area of Iona, so just perhaps, a direct link to someone who may have followed Oswald in his adventure to recover his father's kingdom and stayed on as a warrior at court!

Hostages were also a common thing, with sons of important foreign nobles handed over as kind of collateral for allegiance or good behaviour. We know from poetry that hostages of high status would be well treated at court, eat at the royal table and also fight for the lord that held them, as a bond of honour. The Northumbrian court's political connections to Scotland, Ireland and southern England should be no surprise. Other friendlier alliances may be based on royal and noble marriage and this might well involve connections overseas, as well as within the British Isles. The treasures unearthed at Sutton Hoo had connections far afield - from the similarities of the helmet to those found in Eastern Sweden to the Byzantine bowls. Early medieval royal courts had diplomatic, trading and exchange, links far beyond their frontiers. It seems that people, as well as things, moved more freely than we might have imagined. This along with the possibility of trade could be the main driver behind the presence of a number of Scandinavian signatures in the isotope data.

The other reason we have to explain the far travelled individuals in our cemetery is Christianity and pilgrimage. The conversion of the kingdom to Christianity connected the Northumbrian royal court to a Europe wide network of monasteries and churches and we know from the written evidence that churchmen were often far travelled. Each bishop was expected to visit Rome to receive their pallium (a vestment like a broad cloth band bestowed by the Pope as a symbol of office and authority) and some senior churchmen, such as St Wilfrid, are known to have travelled more than once and were accompanied by a full household of followers. One of the early Archbishops of Canterbury, Theodore of Tarsus (archbishop from AD 668 to 690) was Greek, showing the cosmopolitan nature of the church even then. Pilgrimage, along well established routes to major cult centres, would have been a strong motivation for those with the wherewithal to travel and cover long distances over difficult roads and stormy seas - risking bandits and bad weather. The fact that we have a group of individuals, whose oxygen signature was of a temperature expected from the central or southern Mediterranean, is hard to explain in any other way than the Christian church and the pilgrim routes of Europe. Christianity may be the link that explains why Western Ireland and Western Scotland are so well represented as well. Irish Christianity was instrumental in the Northumbrian conversion and remained important even after the Synod of Whitby in AD 664 when the Northumbrian court turned to Rome as the official court church.

The other distant region that was represented in the isotope data was Scandinavia. This is a region that in the seventh and eighth century cannot be explained away by Christianity and pilgrimage as the region certainly lay outside of Christian Europe at that time. Too early to be seen as a characteristic of the Viking Age we must look at trade and connections that may have continued from the age of migration that occurred at the end of the Roman Empire. Certainly, it has long been believed that the Viking raids, one of the earliest of course being the attack on Lindisfarne in AD 793, cannot have just occurred out of the blue and was in fact a change in a connected trade network that had long been in existence. Here in our burial ground it seems we have evidence for this.

Story One – The Hebridean connections

One burial that has had a fascination from almost the beginning of the excavation is a robust older male from the original evaluation. He was subjected to wide analysis, including an isotope study, radiocarbon dating and skeletal analysis. He was seen as very intriguing because this evidence seemed to fit him quite closely to history. The radiocarbon date suggested a date of death between AD 574 – 660 and a knife and buckle set with the body with a style of knife consistent with the seventh century. This gave an overlap of a few decades in the early to mid

The Hebridean Man – codeword 'Oferbrædan' on the Bamburgh Bones digital ossuary
© G. Young

seventh century, that really became significant when the isotope data suggested that he had grown up in the area of the Hebrides. This fits in well with the story of Oswald and his exile and connections with Iona (one of the Hebridean Islands). Could this older male have been a warrior who had returned with Oswald to serve at his court and who was later interred at the capital of his new chosen kingdom. Of course the evidence falls a little short of full proof but it is consistent and at the least quite likely.

Story Two- the strong Western Scotland and Irish connections

The isotope analysis revealed a considerable number of the burials had childhood origins in Ireland or the West of Scotland. The one obvious connection to these areas is the Christian Church that had been established by Oswald and his conversion in exile. Bede then tells us of the churchmen who came to Northumbria and were so influential in establishing the early monasteries and converting the populace. Here then we have direct evidence of just how close and extensive those connections were. The new results do add one dimension we don't see in the texts as we have quite a few females amongst

The Irish Lady - codeword 'Bæć-Bord' on the Bamburgh Bones digital ossuary © G. Young

them. A half of the population that the male authors of monastic chronicles so often miss out of the tale recovered by modern archaeology. A story in itself.

Story Three – the southern connections

The last really fascinating group are those with very high temperature indication from the Oxygen data that suggests a childhood as far south as the Mediterranean. As with the Irish connection it seems almost certain that we are seeing the church as the reason behind this and it is interesting to note that the two are generally in different parts of the cemetery and the Mediterranean signatures seem to be later in date. Again quite in line with the history of the Northumbria church where we see a turn towards Rome after the Synod of Whitby in AD 664 that led to a great reduction in the number of

The Continental Child – codeword 'Bord' on the Bamburgh Bones digital ossuary © G. Young

Irish churchmen present but not an end to all such connections it seems. Again we see that the connections included women and children and so our burial ground seems to consistently show how history distorts the story through the eyes of male chroniclers.

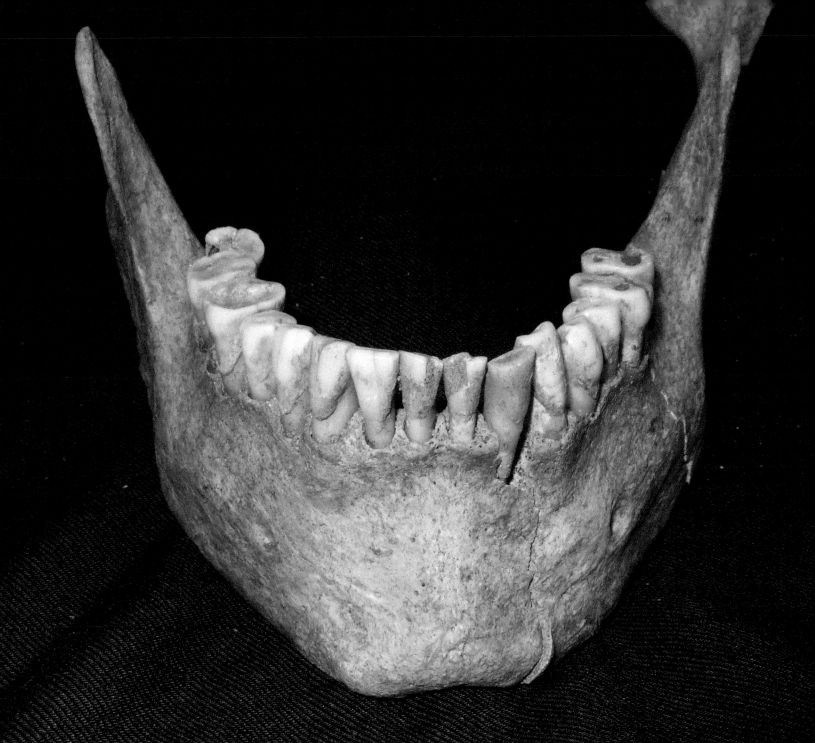

Bowl hole mandible
© C. Roberts

Dance of death Fresco, Clusone, Italy

Reading the bones.
Giving a voice to the people
buried at Bamburgh

Professor Charlotte Roberts

Professor Emeritus Charlotte Roberts has studied archaeological human remains for nearly 40 years. She also has a background in archaeology and nursing (her former profession). She particularly focuses on patterns of health and disease in the past (palaeopathology), and especially those health problems that are common today (e.g. infections such as tuberculosis). More details of her research can be found at www.dur.ac.uk/directory/profile/?id=163.

Introduction

When a cemetery is excavated the first thing we want to know is what the skeletons tell us about who was buried there. This is no different at Bamburgh for the Bowl Hole cemetery. The skeletons were excavated between 1999 and 2007 by the Bamburgh Research Project because the North Sea was eroding the sand dunes where these early medieval people had been laid to rest between the 7th and 9th centuries AD (middle part of the early medieval period). This sort of excavation can be classed as rescue archaeology, which aims to save threatened heritage sites. The Bowl Hole cemetery is unique in several ways; there are few cemeteries of this date in England; there are few cemeteries of any period in north-east England; coastal sites of this period are rare; and the Bowl Hole cemetery is linked to the royal centre that was Bamburgh at that time.

Studying skeletons from archaeological cemeteries are the closest we can get to those once living people who created our past, but we must be mindful of ethical considerations of excavating, analysing, storing and displaying human remains. In any study of human remains it is imperative that the remains are treated with respect and dignity, as was the case for the skeletons that are the subject of this booklet. The skeletons from the Bowl Hole cemetery were originally the subject of a large Arts and Humanities Research Council funded project that ran from 2006 to 2010. It addressed issues of early Medieval cultural contact, population movement, status relations and religious change. We wanted to gain a better understanding of the regional origins, relative status and lifestyle of the people buried at the Bowl Hole, and to explore correlations between the cemetery archaeology, and historical sources relating to the early Anglo-Saxon royal site at Bamburgh. It was an unparalleled opportunity to conduct a detailed study of this cemetery in its local and regional context and in relation to the excavations at Bamburgh Castle. Apart from wanting to know more about these people overall, the following were some of the questions we wanted to specifically answer:

- What were the childhood origins of the people buried here?

- Could 'non-locals' be distinguished from 'locals'?

- Were 'locals' healthier than 'non-locals'

- Did people who were locally born and raised live longer, and were there differences between the sex, age and status groups?

- Did ancient DNA survive in the skeletons that might be used for further studies (it did, but no further work was done!)?

The skeletons were originally recorded by Dr Sarah Groves, who was employed on the project as a postdoctoral research assistant. Following a detailed study they are now reburied within the crypt of St Aidan's Church Bamburgh, as part of the National Lottery Heritage Fund project Accessing Aidan, but their lives live on in the form of the Digital Ossuary open to all.

How many skeletons were there?

There were 98 individual skeletons excavated between 1999 and 2007, but like many cemeteries there was also a lot of extra bones found amongst the individual burials. Excavation was carefully done to make sure all the bones of each were recovered because this is important when it comes to analysis, especially when trying to work out what health problems these people had when they were living. The skeletons were cleaned before they were analysed. Preservation of the bones of each skeleton varied, from ones that were almost complete to others that were only represented by a few bones. Almost half of the skeletons had 90% of their bones excavated. The better-preserved ones were buried in the sandy soil of the dunes, while poorly preserved ones were excavated from deeper graves in clay.

Were there men, women and children buried in the cemetery, and how old were they when they died?

The majority of the skeletons were adults (71), and most of the non-adults were aged 1 year or older at death. A third of the adults were older (46 years or older). Thirty-seven of them were males and 28 were females; six of the adults could not be assigned a sex because the pelvic and skull bones that are used to estimate sex were not preserved. It is not possible to work out the sex of skeletons of people who were not adults either, so we can only guess whether the 27 non-adults were girls or boys, or their genders. However, ancient DNA analysis can be used determine the sex of a young person. Note that the term sex is different to gender; sex is a biological term and gender refers to the social characteristics of women and men that are socially constructed – a person may be born a biological male or female but assume a particular gender. Sometimes we find graves which contain a male or female skeleton with grave goods that suggest the opposite (e.g. a woman buried with a weapon); we can then start to think about the nature of gender identity in the past. Of interest are the 11 skeletons of young people whose bones seemed to have grown slowly compared to the age estimated from their teeth. Teeth are more reliable age markers, but the growth of bones can be affected by childhood disease or an insufficient diet. All of these children were less than 14 years of age and they all had markers of "stress" in their bones and teeth. This shows that they did experience either poor health or problems with what they were eating when their bones were growing.

Peculiaritics in bones and teeth

Sometimes the bones and teeth of people's skeletons reveal 'peculiarities' (or 'non-metric traits'). These are not due to disease but reflect either something they have inherited (like extra bones – or ossicles -in the joints (sutures) of the skull, or the effect of being physically active (like markers on joints due to adopting a squatting posture - squatting facets). The ones that are inherited can help us understand the mobility or movement of people. These peculiarities are more or less common in different parts of the world.

Therefore, if a person buried in a particular cemetery has a trait that is very common somewhere else then it can be suggested that this person moved from that place during their lives, and were buried away from their birthplace in a cemetery containing people who were raised in the local area and did not move during their life and had lower frequencies of the trait. Along with chemical (or stable isotope) analysis, this can provide a strong argument for people moving across landscapes. Fifty per cent of females and 39% of the males had wormian bones in their skull, suggesting that there were quite a few related people buried in the Bowl Hole cemetery. Interestingly, there were quite a few people of both sexes who had squatting facets on their lower leg bone (shin or tibia), suggesting they adopted this posture regularly, perhaps in the work that they did. When looking at these peculiarities in the teeth, which are believed to be inherited, one stood out and was present in over half of the individuals with preserved teeth. This was 'shovelling' of the incisor teeth, a feature that is most common in Asian populations today. Whether the people at Bamburgh had some genes of Asian origin, we will never know.

Shovelling of the incisor teeth

This is one of many 'dental non-metric traits' that can be present on the teeth of people in the past and the present. They are thought to be inherited through the family. Therefore, features in the teeth are of interest because they can be used to identify people who migrated from distant parts of the globe and were buried well away from "home". Some people buried at Bamburgh had what is called shovelling of the incisor teeth (the tongue side of the incisor teeth are 'scooped out'). Today, this is known to be associated with people who live in Asia or who are native American. That said, this can be seen in the teeth people who did not originate in Asia, although they are not common in Europeans. However, as we have isotope evidence at Bamburgh of people originating outside of England, we have to keep an open mind.

Health and well-being

In general terms, the people buried at Bamburgh were quite healthy, although that is a rather simplistic statement! Of course, today people can live with multiple diseases and still feel pretty well and healthy, not least due to advances in "care", and a range of treatment options, including drug therapy and surgery. Therefore, "health" will have different definitions for individual people in different cultures. This may well be related to diseases they have (which may not be actually causing and signs or symptoms suggesting "illness"), but also to their general living conditions that make them feel unhealthy, like being hungry. We will never know the full range of health problems these people had because all we have are their skeletons to tell us their life stories, and many more diseases affect the soft tissues than the bones and teeth. For example, today cardiovascular disease is the leading cause of death in Britain, but deaths from Alzheimer's disease are increasing; neither affect the skeleton in a way we can recognize them. Low levels of physical activity, obesity, binge drinking, and the long-term effects of smoking are clearly impacting health too, and there are also differences in health between people due to inequalities, particularly related to poor education and low income. We also know that inequalities existed in the past that would have led to poor health. This was especially so in urban medieval communities where life was not necessarily like the idyllic image we have for people living in the countryside like those buried at Bamburgh. Living in natural environments, including on the coast, has been described as beneficial to physical and mental health, and the coast has been a draw for healing and treatment for centuries, including inhaling the fresh air, and coastal towns attracts retirees! Cold water bathing has also been recommended and of course has come very much back into fashion in recent times ('wild swimming'). To understand whether living at Bamburgh during the 7th–9th centuries AD was healthier than at other places needs to be explored.

In the early medieval period when the Bowl Hole cemetery was being used, we would expect to see dental disease, trauma, joint disease, infections, and maybe some deficiency diseases like scurvy and anaemia. We perhaps would not expect to see cancer as much as we see it today, or even heart disease, and one wonders when/if Alzheimers disease was a condition that our ancestors experienced. In any case, all these diseases mainly affect the soft tissues. Diagnosis of disease in archaeological skeletons is fraught with challenges, with the constant reminder that even in western society where there are many diagnostic tests, including taking a history of feeling unwell from the patient, diagnoses can be very hard to reach.

Smelly mouths?

As expected, dental diseases were common, but more so that we might expected in this population. Chemical analysis of their teeth showed that they were eating a diet that included seafood. Fish flesh and bones contain fluoride, which can protect the teeth from becoming rotten, but that did not seem to be the case for the people buried at Bamburgh. Dental infections were common and included rotten teeth due to eating a diet too full of sugar (caries) and abscesses (infection on the roots of teeth), along with plaque (the stuff your dentist wants you to get rid of), and defects in the white tooth enamel surface that indicate "stress" during development of the teeth (enamel hypoplasia). Having a childhood disease like measles, mumps or whooping cough or eating a diet that lacked essential foodstuffs can lead to these defects, which are etched on the permanent teeth for life. The milk teeth may also be affected. If people had caries, they must not have been eating enough fish to counteract the consumption of a lot of sugar. While they relied on farmed food like cereal crops that contained sugar, and probably ate fruits that naturally contain sugar,

they were likely consuming other sugary products like honey or even mead (an alcoholic drink of fermented honey and water). This drink has a long history of production on nearby Holy Island going back to monastic communities who settled there in the 7th century AD.

Plaque, or more properly called calculus when it has become hard, was by far the most common problem affecting the teeth of people buried

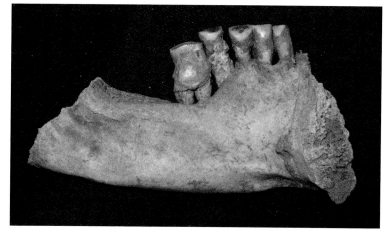

A large amount of plaque on a molar tooth © C. Roberts

at Bamburgh. Interesting work on dental calculus tells us that inside it lots of things might be preserved, including the DNA of disease -causing organisms such as bacteria. Unfortunately, during the time period when the skeletons were being analysed this was not really being done – advances in analytical methods show how much more we could know about these skeletons if we only had had the technology (and money)! There were 58 adults and 20 non-adults that had calculus, suggesting that many people did not clean their teeth. Thirty-six people had rotten teeth and 22 had one or more abscesses; both can be very painful. Enamel defects were recorded in just over half of the adults and in a majority of the non-adults, indicating that living conditions during childhood led to problems in normal development of the teeth. Quite a few people had crowded teeth and some teeth were rotated out of their normal position. While today people can have crowding of their teeth (often corrected by braces), even back in the early medieval period people had jaws that were too short to hold all the 32 permanent teeth, whereas earlier in time this was not seen as much. Eating a softer diet when people's food started to be

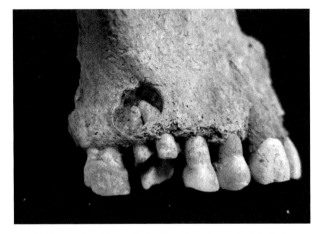

Evidence of a rotten molar tooth and an abscess © C. Roberts

produced by farming has been one explanation because people did not use their chewing muscles as much; hunter-gatherers had to chew their foods much more and therefore their jaws needed to be large and strong. Some of the people also had V shaped notches/grooves in their front teeth (mainly in women), and this might indicate they were using their teeth as tools/as a third hand in some sort of work, for example to soften fibres or wood or to hold thread or twine or leather.

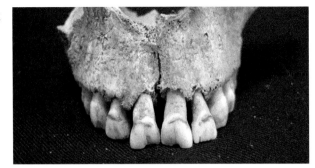

Notches in the front upper teeth, possibly from using the teeth as a tool (e.g. holding plant materials) © C. Roberts

Joint disease: hard work, old age or both?

Many people buried at Bamburgh also had disease of their joints. Joint degeneration is a fact of life; as we grow older our joints essentially wear out. Today, osteoarthritis is the most common joint disease. Being female and/or of older age, having an inherited predisposition, being obese, having an underlying injury, and movement of the joints during activity are all important risk factors. Nearly two-thirds of the adults had evidence for degeneration in the vertebral bodies that make up the spine, more men than women were affected, and the lower (lumbar) spine was more commonly affected. The tiny joints at the back of the spine were less affected. Degeneration of non-spinal joints was also seen. Males were more affected in their shoulders, elbows, wrists, left hand, hips, knee-caps and feet, and females were only affected markedly in their right shoulder, right hip, and right knee. Overall, older people's joints were more affected, as expected, but it would be very difficult to say whether the joint disease was related to physical activity linked to the type of work done during their lives. They would have worked in agriculture, fishing and hunting, and produced household goods like clothes, pottery, and metal products. All these tasks could have taken their toll on people's joints, but older age is strongly linked too. Maybe a combination of age and the impact of work was responsible?

Injury: accidents or aggression?

Injuries include breaks (fractures) to bones and dislocations of joints, where the bones of a joint are forced out of their normal position. Injuries to the soft tissues of the body can also leave their mark on bones where ligaments, tendons and muscles attach. Accidents, underlying stress (e.g. in specific sports like running), and underlying disease like thinning and weakening of the bones (osteoporosis) cause breaks to bones. There are also treatments for injuries that can be identified, like amputation (removal of part of the body like a hand) and trepanation (drilling a hole in the skull). Of course, humans can be violent, and were in the past, and the marks of combat may be seen on the skeleton, like head injuries.

Thirty-two adults had one or more possible indicators of trauma in their upper or lower limbs (nearly 50% of the total number of adults). People's vertebrae and ribs were more injured than the other bones, and men were more affected than women. There was hardly any evidence of head injuries. One young adult male had possible evidence of a perimortem (around the time of death) head injury with no evidence of healing. There was also one very young (18 months to 2-year-old) child, without a head injury, who may have experienced trepanation (surgical removal of a piece of skull). Injury due to combat

Evidence of a healed head injury © C. Roberts

was seen in two male adults, one to the front of their skull and the other to their left ribs, shoulder blade (scapula), upper arm bone (humerus), pelvis, and left thigh bone (femur). There was no evidence of healing of these wounds.

Injuries in the Bamburgh people thus seem to be more related to accidents rather than to conflict, suggesting a relatively peaceful existence for these people in this place. This is despite evidence to suggest that life in eastern England at this time could have been disrupted by migrants from the continent. However, at least two people were probably assaulted, but by who or for what reason will remain unknown.

Evidence of two unhealed injuries on the shoulder joint of a person, caused by a bladed instrument © C. Roberts

Infections: hands, face, and space

While we have no evidence that newly emerging diseases like the recent coronoavirus were around at Bamburgh in the early medieval period, there was evidence for some infectious disease in the bones of the skeletons. Infections can be caused by organisms like viruses, bacteria, fungi, parasitic worms). Many can be passed on from animals to humans, for example via the products of animals, for example food like meat and milk (e.g. tuberculosis). When bones are affected, the inflammation causes new bone to be formed, or bone to be destroyed. There were no skeletons buried in the Bowl Hole cemetery that definitely showed evidence of an infectious disease which we know is caused by, for example, a specific bacteria (e.g. leprosy or tuberculosis). However, evidence of new bone formation as a result of inflammation was seen in some individuals on their ribs, in their sinuses (in the face), and on upper and lower limb bones. Approximately a third of skeletons with preserved leg bones (femur, tibia and fibula) had evidence of inflammation on them, with the upper limb bones not being affected much at all (humerus, radius and ulna). Males more than females were affected. Causes of the inflammation may be infection but, in the case of the tibia (shin bone), injuries sustained in daily life could be responsible. How often do we knock our shin bones? More interesting is the inflammation of the ribs and sinuses, which suggests poor air quality causing respiratory disease. Although the numbers are small, men were more affected than women, and the older age groups more than the younger group.

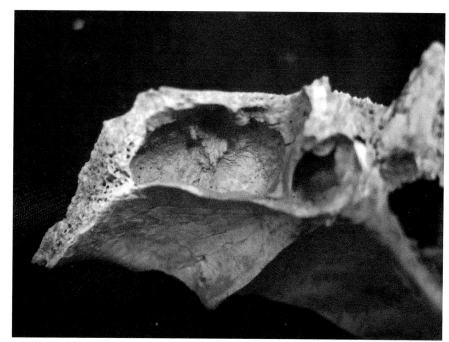

Evidence of sinusitis (spikes of new bone caused by inflammation), possibly caused by poor air quality
© C. Roberts

Very few individuals had rib lesions, indicating that the lungs of these people were generally healthy. We would not expect people living at Bamburgh to have had respiratory problems – fresh sea air, a rural idyll – but we have to remember that their houses were built of wood and had a thatched roof, and they may not have been as clear of pollution as their outside world. Open fires burning wood and other organic matter likely generated particulate matter into the air for people to inhale, and even farming activities outside, like threshing of grain (separating it from the stem), could produce a lot of dust that could cause inflammation of the sinuses and lungs. As we know today, air pollution is a common problem, and caused by so many things; it was also something some of the people living at Bamburgh had to face.

You are what you eat, or are you?

We looked for evidence that the people at Bamburgh were eating a healthy well-balanced diet. The ways in which we can find out about a person's diet is to look for evidence for any deficiencies that affected their bones and teeth. We know they were certainly eating a lot of sugar because of their bad teeth, and during their childhood their diet was probably lacking in some nutrients, like vitamins or minerals, causing the defects in their tooth enamel. However, we can see only what we can see, and there will be people buried at Bamburgh who may have had a deficient diet but died with no markers of that deficiency. Occasionally, we might see evidence of excessive food being consumed, for example in the disease called DISH (diffuse idiopathic skeletal hyperostosis). There were two people

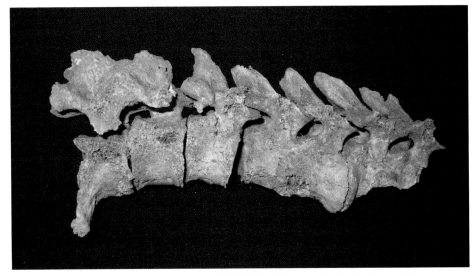

The spine of a person with evidence of possible DISH (spine is fused on the right side), a condition today associated with obesity, diabetes, and a rich diet © C. Roberts

buried in the Bowl Hole cemetery, both older men, with signs of this disease in their spines. Today it is associated with men, older age, obesity, and Type 2 diabetes and in later medieval Britain in monastic communities, although not always. Perhaps these two men ate to excess; they both certainly had a lot of dental disease, including rotten teeth, so sugar must have been on the menu, and maybe mead! At this point we should mention another "excess" disease linked to consumption, gout. Gout affects men more than women and is associated with a high protein diet, high alcohol consumption, heart disease, and high blood pressure, and it can be inherited. The big toe is most affected and people can have much pain, redness and swelling of the joints. A woman and a man seem to have evidence of this disease – more evidence for mead consumption?

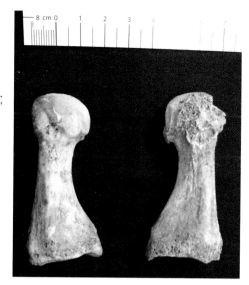

The big toe bones of a person with possible gout
(left is normal and right side is damaged)
© C. Roberts

Other abnormalities found in the Bamburgh skeletons suggesting potential dietary problems included holes in the bone of the eye sockets, likely linked to iron deficiency. Iron deficiency anaemia is a serious global public health problem, according to the World Health Organization. However, there are many causes of iron deficiency, such as infection or injury leading to excessive blood loss, gut problems like bowel cancer, or a deficiency of components of the diet, for example iron or vitamin B12, found variously in fish, meat, poultry, eggs, dairy products and certain vegetables. About one third of adults had this condition (more men than women), but nearly half of the 19 non-adults were affected. What specifically caused this is unknown, but some dietary deficiency seems likely, considering other evidence like those enamel defects described earlier. Anaemia can cause tiredness, headaches, dizziness, breathlessness, and palpitations.

Holes in the eye socket indicating anaemia © C. Roberts

As for deficiencies of specific vitamins or minerals, there was very little evidence. One young woman at Bamburgh may have had scurvy, or vitamin C deficiency. A lack of fresh fruit and vegetables is usually the cause, and young children and older people are usually affected today. Bleeding into the skin and the gums, loss of teeth, pain, bruising, anaemia and poor wound healing may occur. Another person may have had vitamin D deficiency when they were a child, as shown by their bent leg bones; rickets remains a challenge globally and is linked to many other diseases, like those affecting the lungs. Vitamin D is formed in the skin as a result mainly of ultraviolet light skin exposure, but dietary sources high in the vitamin also contribute to a person's "intake" (e.g. oily fish). 15-20 minutes exposure is meant to be sufficient in the summer months to generate enough of the vitamin, but people with dark skins need twice that exposure. Covering the skin with clothes and using high factor sun cream can prevent UV rays "hitting" the skin. Vitamin D is essential for getting calcium and phosphorus into the bones during childhood to mineralize them. If vitamin D is not readily available then the bones will bend under pressure when a child starts to crawl and walk. It is quite surprising to see this vitamin deficiency at Bamburgh because it would be expected that most people got exposure to UV light on a daily basis (and have access to oily fish). However, we should be mindful that vitamin D deficiency today in Britain rises the further north you live. Bamburgh is on the same latitude as Denmark to the east and Canada to the west, and during the winter UV light is more limited than further south because of shorter daylight hours.

Were Bamburgh people on the move? What can their teeth tell us?

Early Medieval England is described historically as a time when people migrated from the Continent to English shores. In fact, the Benedictine monk, the Venerable Bede, who lived during the 7th/8th century AD in the Kingdom of Northumbria talked of migrants flocking into eastern England and displacing the local native people. A key question is the extent to which cultural changes seen in the early medieval period were due to movement of people or ideas, or both. We did a study to see if the people buried in the Bowl Hole cemetery were non-locally born and came to Bamburgh because of its royal status. The way we did this was to take small samples of enamel from the teeth of the skeletons to produce strontium and oxygen isotope ratios/values.

Variations in geological and environmental conditions create combinations of stable isotopes that can be distinctive to particular geographic regions, and these isotopes are present in food (strontium) and water (oxygen), and become incorporated into bones and teeth during their development. The composition and age of the underlying bedrock (strontium), and topography, altitude, climate, and rainfall in a region determines the values. Where a person has migrated from their place of birth or childhood origin, the strontium and oxygen isotopic signatures of their tooth enamel may differ significantly from that of their place of burial – but similar values can be found in different regions where the bedrock and water are the same. That's how we find migrants in skeletons buried in an ancient cemetery like the Bowl Hole but, like anything, it's complicated!

The results showed that non-local people comprised the majority of those buried in the cemetery, with many from other parts of Britain; the royal status of the Castle, the seat of the kings of Northumbria, and its political and religious power was probably the "draw"! Several male, female, and nonadult individuals had "non-local" isotopic signatures, and some had childhood origins in Scandinavian countries. There was also a separate group with signatures that suggested origins in the southern Mediterranean or North Africa. Migration was not restricted to men; both men, women and children were all present in both the potentially "Scandinavian" and "Southern European" groups. There were also differences in health between local and migrant groups. However, these differences did not seem to extend to burial practices and there were no clear links between a regional origin and burial position or the types of artefacts placed in the grave, other than a slight tendency for non-locals and non-UK individuals to be buried in a prone position (face down). It is well known that the mobility of people can impact their health today and that people travel for a variety of reasons, for example, to escape danger and to gain a better life, among others. However, their health can be challenged by moving place of residence; they may encounter diseases their immune systems have not experienced before, but they may also bring diseases with them. They may experience poor health because their living conditions may be compromised as migrants. Thus, exploring the impact of mobility on people's health and well-being, by comparing the health of locally born and raised people with those who migrated from elsewhere may provide an indication of relative health of migrants and non-migrants. For example, a comparison of height between the groups of local, nonlocal, and non-UK individuals identified differences in between groups with different origins. Males of possible Scandinavian origin were taller on average than all other men; and "local" women, or those who had been born in the greater region of Northumbria, were on average the shortest. This difference may be caused by the different genetic makeup of these groups, but may also reflect differences in nutrition and quality of life during childhood, perhaps indicating that people who were able to migrate to Bamburgh were of higher social status and had a better quality of life than those who were locally born. As this study showed, it is clear that movement across early Medieval Europe was not uncommon for the political and religious elite. Bamburgh also served as a hub for trade, politics and religious contact.

Early medieval life expectancy

The skeletons of the people buried at Bamburgh revealed that the majority of the adults were "older", as far as our age estimation methods allowed us to infer (age estimation into old age groups is difficult); this proportion is higher than at some other contemporary sites. However, about a quarter of those buried there had not reached adulthood, including three who had died around the time of birth, but the proportion of non-adult skeletons at some other sites is much higher. This suggests that life could be tough during the growing years for many, and at other early medieval cemetery sites evidence shows that females died during childbirth (female skeletons with foetal bones associated with them in the grave). Overall, the information shows that if a person survived the early years they could expect to live to a 'decent age'. This indicates that health and well-being at Bamburgh during adulthood seems to have been conducive to a good quality of life.

Conclusions

The detailed study of the Bowl Hole cemetery skeletons will be published as a monograph with British Archaeological Reports in due course. This will be the result of a long-term study funded by the Arts and Humanities Research Council. Durham University is grateful for the opportunity to do this study, a study that contributes to a dearth of studies of early medieval cemeteries of this date anywhere and particularly in north-east England. It has allowed us to give voices to the people buried in the Bowl Hole cemetery for them to tell their story, a fascinating story at that! The skeletons now lie in peace within the crypt of St. Aidan's Church at Bamburgh as part of the Heritage Lottery Funded project Accessing Aidan, but their lives live on in the form of a "Digital Ossuary" open to all (bamburghbones.org). Do explore this ossuary to learn more and see the final resting place of the people who were buried at Bamburgh. The rows of ossuary (skeleton) boxes, each containing human bones, is a memorable but also a sobering reminder of our own mortality.

Further reading

Brothwell D 1981 *Digging up bones*. London, British Museum (Natural History).

Mays S 2010 *The archaeology of human bones*. 2nd edition. London, Routledge.

Roberts CA 2018 *Human remains in archaeology. A handbook*. 2nd edition. York, CBA.

Roberts CA, Cox M 2003 *Health and disease in Britain: prehistory to the present day*. Gloucester, Sutton Publishing.

Roberts C, Manchester K 2005 *The archaeology of disease*. 3rd edition. Stroud, Sutton Publishing.

Sayer D 2010 *Ethics and burial archaeology*. London, Duckworth.

Ethics and human remains in archaeology

As living people we are all individuals and will have varying opinions about how archaeological human remains should be treated.

Some feel that excavated human remains should all be stored for future research following initial analysis. On the other hand, others feel that once analyzed, the remains should be reburied. In between those extremes, there are those who believe a balance has to be struck between paying due respect to those we study while giving these once-living people a voice through analyzing them, but also accepting that there are times and places when human remains should be reburied or restricted from certain analyses.

We must also be mindful that because we cannot gain permission from the dead to excavate, analyze, curate and display them, we must treat them with all the dignity and respect we can apply. They are not the same as other things we excavate like pottery or animal bones – they are the remains of once-living people like you. The Bowl Hole skeletons were fully analyzed during a research project between 2006 and 2010, from recording their sex and age at death and estimating height (stature) to looking at their health and well being and their origins and diet using stable isotope analysis. Following this project, it was therefore appropriate that the skeletons were laid to rest in the crypt of St. Aidan's Church at Bamburgh, close to where they were found.

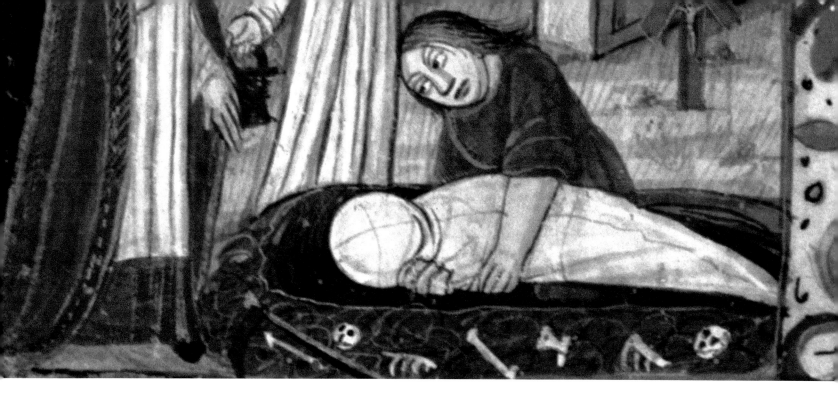

Ossuaries

Jessica Turner

*Jessica Turner is the Accessing Aidan Project Officer and works for the Northumberland Coast
AONB Partnership. She has a background in Field Archaeology and Historic Environment
Advice in designated landscapes and more latterly has developed a keen interest in the early
Christian heritage of the Northumberland Coast.*

What is an ossuary?

An ossuary is a vessel that contains human bone and can vary from an individual box – such as the infamous 'James Ossuary' - to a room, a crypt or building to store a communal collection of human bones. Ossuaries are also referred to as Charnel Houses.

The development of Ossuaries

Ossuaries in Europe date from the early to middle 1200s and their establishment as a part of the ecclesiastical architecture must have been in part due theological teaching but also a necessity in response to overcrowding in cemeteries. Christain teaching was that the immortal soul resided in the mortal human body until death, and it was then that the soul that ascends to heaven. Whilst the concept of the soul predates Christianity, the goodness, or otherwise, of a person's soul and their eventual acceptance into heaven was a very important preoccupation of early Christain teachings, for example in around AD 400 St Augustine recorded his mother's, St Monica, intersessions for the redemption of his soul.

Funeral in the Middle Age - a miniature from a 15th century Book of Hours, France - showing the bones in soil from the freshly dug grave. Photo © CCI / Bridgeman Images

Christianity was officially adopted across Europe in AD 380 by the Roman Empire. The prevailing burial practice in the fourth century Roman Britain was typically inhumations outside the settlement limits along routeways. As with much early Christain practice it is thought that many traditions evolved from or adapted rites and rituals of the previously pagan religion. Funerary tradition would have been no different and is accepted that post Roman cemeteries continued to be outside the settlement. However, by the AD 800 there was a move for Christain burials to be on consecrated ground. Ground could be, and still is, consecrated by a bishop and traditionally was the plot of land surrounding a church. So, by 1200 continual burial in the same enclosed space for about 400 years had resulted in overcrowding, particularly given that grave markers were not commonplace. Bones were inevitably disturbed by the cutting of new graves particularly during the latter part of this period. This posed an interesting dilemma for the church, it was accepted that the holy immortal soul had departed its earthly vessel, but the body remains holy in anticipation of the Resurrection and disturbing a body was considered an abominable act. In the early 1200s the church reconciled the conflict between continual burial and keeping the faithful departed on consecrated ground by creating Ossuaries.

Archangel Michael and the souls in purgatory
© sedmak/123RF.com

Interestingly, at around the same time at the Second Council of Lyon in AD 1274, Pope Gregory X formalised the church's teaching concerning Purgatory. Purgatory was not a new concept, again St Augustine had written about it in the early 400s, but there was no formal doctrine. In 1274 it was decreed that Purgatory existed and that it was an intermediary place for the soul's of "all who die in God's grace and friendship but still imperfectly purified" to be cleansed for entry to heaven. How long one's soul would reside in Purgatory depended greatly on the scale of one's lifelong imperfections and how long it took to purge the sins. The 2nd Council set out two points – that some souls could be purified after death and more importantly that 'such souls benefit from the prayers and pious duties that the living do for them'. Is it a coincidence that moving human bones into a communal space and the concept of pious duties by the living could help expedite the dearly departed's time in Purgatory became a theologically accepted doctrine at the same time? Perhaps it is too cynical to suggest that the Purgatory teaching enabled the monetisation of the charnelling business, but it certainly resulted in some 'pious acts' having an economic value. Ossuaries and Charnel Houses certainly represented the collective endeavour of a community, but the tradition was borne out of chantries and private endowments to the church from the wealthiest in society that start to appear in the 1100s. Usually stipulated as part of a will, funds were set aside to build a chantry and to employ one or more priests to sing a stipulated number of services for the benefit of the soul of a specified deceased person. The creation of charnel houses and ossuaries must have brought mortality sharply into focus and the prospect of an indeterminable time in Purgatory cannot have been an appetising notion. So communally a priest could be employed to pray for the souls of all those in the ossuary. This act of 'pious duty' could potentially benefit the souls of the departed but might also mitigate some of ones own imperfections in anticipation.

Sedlec Ossuary in the Czech Republic, the Capuchin Crypt in Rome and the Chapel of Bones at Evora in Portugul are amongst some of the best known ossuaries in Europe. The fame of these three ossuaries could be, in part, due to the imaginative way that the variety of bones of the human skeletons have been used to decorate these sacred spaces – for example at Sedlec the chandeliers are constructed of vertebrae, humerus and pelvis. The Capuchins in Rome use, together with fully dressed whole skeletons, the scapulas to create the illusion of angel wings around skull and at Evora the bones are used to look like an integral part of the building's structure. These are wonderous places and well worth a visit.

Ordinarily ossuaries do not tend to hold the whole skeleton. In reality the exhumation of a human

Detail of the interior of the Sedlec Ossuary, Kutna Hora in the Czech Republic © C. Roberts

The Chapel of Bones, Evora, Portugal © bloodua/123RF.com

skeleton is quite difficult, there are 213 bones in an adult skeleton and 270 in an infant varying from the strong sturdy femur (thigh bone) to the tiny bones in the inner ear (malleus, incus and stapes). Many ossuaries are dominated by the femurs and skulls – these being the strongest, robust and most readily identifiable bones in the skeleton and easily retrived from the cemetery. These are also the two of the most diagnostically useful bones as from these bones it is possible to work out how tall, how old and which gender the person was. The practice evolved that the skull and the femur was sufficient to represent the person as a whole and in fact the origin of the skull and crossbones and why this symbol was often used as a memento mori on tombstones in the late Medieval period - this is rather more prosaic reason than the common misinterpretation of pirate graves.

The Paris catacomb is a good example of the storage of femurs and skulls. Some parts of the Paris catacomb date from the Roman period but the space was not utilised as a repository for bones from the overcrowded city cemeteries until the 18th century. Undoubtedly the most poignant ossuary in France is the Douaumont Ossuary located close to the WWI battlefield of Verdun which holds the bones of at least 130,000 unidentified soldiers.

Charnelling, the process of moving bones into a charnel box or ossuary, is still practiced to certain extent in Italy and Greece. Ossuaries can also be found in the Near East, but also in Mexico and North America, and they are often related to both Catholic and Orthodox faiths.

Top: Paris Catacombs
© lindrik/123RF.COM

Bottom: The Douaumont Ossuary at the site of the
Battle of Verdun

English Ossuaries

Given the evolution of ossuaries in the 1200s it is reasonable to assume that Ossuaries were commonplace in Britain, both documentary and archaeological evidence attests to this fact, but the 16th century Reformation saw this very catholic tradition go quickly out of favour in Britain, as it did in many northern European countries as the protestant religious reform took hold.

A good example of an English Ossuary is the Spitalfields Charnel House excavated by the Museum of London in 1999. The free-standing charnel house once stood in the grounds of St Mary Spital, a medieval hospital site at Bishopsgate in the city of London. The remains of standing walls vary between 1m-3m high are now on permanent display and survived because the charnel house had been reused to create a cellar of a 16th century townhouse, bizarrely a small pile of ancient bones survived in situ in one corner of the room.

Remarkably there are still two intact medieval ossuaries in England – Holy Trinity Church at Rothwell in

Rothwell Bone Crypt at Holy Trinity Church, Rothwell, Northamptonshire
© Chris Tweed

Northamptonshire and St Leonard's in Hythe, Kent. It is believed that both ossuary crypts had been closed and earthed up at the time of the Reformation and were forgotten about.

St Leonards Ossuary comprises of neatly stacked skulls on shelves with femurs stacks further into the room. It is estimated that there are about 1200 skulls in the crypt. Holy Trintiy also has shelves of skulls and is perhaps not as asthetically neat as St Leonards as the central space contain jumbles of fermurs, it is estimated that the bones assemblage represents about 2,500 individuals.

St Leonard's Ossuary, Hythe, Kent
© Ian Hadingham

In addition to Holy Trinity and St Leonard's there is a post-medieval ossuary at St. Bride's, Fleet Street, London. The late dates of the interment in this ossuary in 1665 and 1854 relate to the great Plague and Cholera epidemic respectively and illustrates that overcrowding in a cemetery was a continual issue.

The Bamburgh Ossuary © Andy Gardner Web Design

Burial Positions

Supine: lying on the back with the face or front upward – this is perceived as the most usual position for a Christian burial but only really becomes the norm after about AD 900.

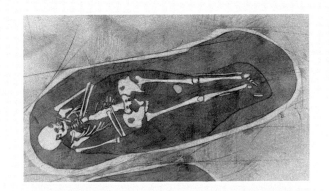

Prone: lying on the front with the back of the head upwards - possible explanations vary from a show of humility in anticipation of the Resurrection, or that the deceased was not worthy of facing the Second Coming so placed in an already penitent position or perhaps carelessness on the part of those burying the body.

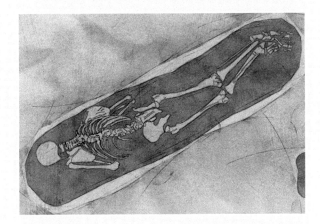

Crouch: usually side on, with the bent legs tucked up to the chest – possibly a holdover of various burial traditions that predate the conventional Christian tradition. This does not mean that they represent non-Christian burials, but rather the Bowl hole cemetary was in use before standard burial practice was formalised.

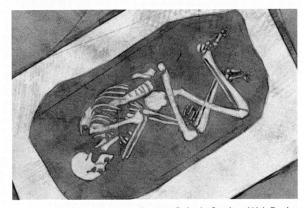

Images © Andy Gardner Web Design

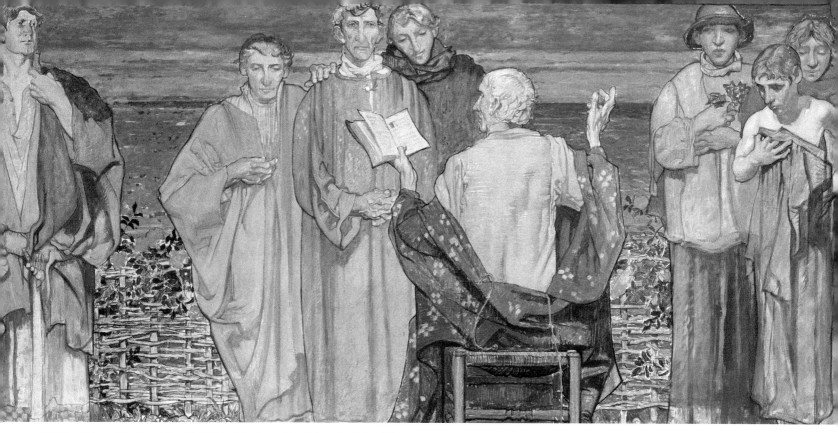

St Aidan, Bishop of Northumbria, A.D. 635, training boys at Lindisfarne by Sir Frank Brangwyn
Reproduced here by the kind permission of David Brangwyn and Christ's Hospital

Aidan: a saint for our times

John Connell

John Connell is the author of The Man Who Gave His Horse to a Beggar, the most lavishly-illustrated biography of Aidan of Lindisfarne ever produced. A former newspaper reporter from Alnmouth in Northumberland, he is now employed as the senior caseworker (and speech writer) for the Member of Parliament for Workington, Cumbria. John has an MA in Medieval Studies from the University of York where he specialised in the material culture and religious iconography of Golden Age Northumbria.

When the Northumbrian prince Oswald fled his homeland with his war-widowed mother, he was a whey-faced boy in fear of his life. He returned a battle-hardened warrior who had seen action in Ireland fighting for his Gaelic-speaking hosts. Groomed for kingship during almost two decades of exile in what is now western Scotland, he was now every inch the early medieval warlord. The monks of the famous Hebridean monastery of Iona and the kings of the Dál Riata who had taken him under their wing had high hopes. Now, at long last, the opportunity had arrived for him to step into the breach. He did not disappoint.

Oswald surprised his enemies in an audacious dawn raid, driving them before him in a bloody rout. The battle started at Heavenfield [NY 937 696] in the shadow of Hadrian's Wall, less than five miles from Hexham in Northumberland. This is the stuff from which legends are made: a king forced into exile reclaims his rightful throne and delivers his people. The Welsh king who had killed Oswald's half-brother, Eanfrith, in cold blood and ravaged his people lay dead in the dirt. This decisive victory against Cadwallon, in the year AD 633 or AD 634, not only made Oswald the most powerful man in Britain overnight: it was also the catalyst for a revolution that forever changed the religious and cultural landscape of the North.

As it is for so much of our early medieval history (a period controversially described by some as the 'Dark Ages'), our main source for what happened next is Bede's *Ecclesiastical History of the English People (EH)*, written in around AD 731:

> *"Oswald, as soon as he had come to the throne, was anxious that the whole race under his rule should be filled with the grace of the Christian faith of which he had so wonderful an experience in overcoming the barbarians. So he sent to the Irish elders among whom he and his thegns had received the sacrament of baptism when he was in exile. He requested them to send a bishop by whose teaching and ministry the English race over whom he ruled might learn the privileges of faith in our Lord and receive the sacraments. His request was granted without delay." EH III. 3*

It was quite natural that Oswald should look to the Irish to convert his countrymen rather than to the Roman missionaries active elsewhere in Britain. He had spent almost two decades living in the Gaelic-speaking kingdom of Dál Riata, which straddled the northern part of Ireland and the western seaboard of Scotland. The religious centre of this sea kingdom was the island monastery of Iona founded by the great Saint Columba (AD 521 – AD 597). It is here that Oswald received instruction while he grew to manhood, becoming fully imbued in the traditions of Celtic monasticism. And because the missionary drive came from this direction rather than from Rome, the brand of Christianity brought to Northumbria had a slightly different flavour to the form being introduced among the more southerly Anglo-Saxon kingdoms.

The distinction may appear abstruse to us today. Put very simply and crudely, the Roman and the Irish camps did not agree on when to celebrate Easter and over the form of the monastic tonsure – the way monks cut their hair. There were cultural differences as well as variations in practice and emphasis between these loose groupings. The Irish had a different system of penance and placed greater emphasis upon 'going into exile for Christ' (retreating from the world to become monks, pilgrims or hermits) while the Roman Church was perhaps more clerical, hierarchical and centralised. These divisions would not come to a head until AD 664 – more than a decade after Aidan's death – when Oswald's brother and successor Oswiu convened the Synod of Whitby to decide once and for all which side would prevail.

The first mission from Iona to Northumbria was not a success. Led by a man named in later sources as Corman, Bede notes his harsh and austere approach. This did not endear him to the Anglo-Saxon Northumbrian people, many of whom still worshipped the old gods of the Germanic pantheon including the likes of Thunor and Woden (more commonly known to us today by their Norse names of Thor and Odin). Shuffling back to his own people on Iona, defeated and frustrated, the monk was unwilling to accept responsibility for his failure and laid the blame firmly at the door of the barbarous English. Reporting back to a conference of elders, he told them that he had been unable to make headway because his hosts were *"intractable, obstinate and uncivilised"*. There ensued a long and anxious discussion about what to do next, until one of their number broke the deadlock and presented a solution:

"It seems to me, brother, that you have been unreasonably harsh upon your ignorant hearers: you did not first offer them the milk of simpler teaching, as the apostle recommends, until little by little, as they grew strong on the food of God's word, they were capable of receiving more elaborate instruction and of carrying out the more transcendent commandments of God." (EH III.5)

The speaker's name was Aidan and, based on the strength of this interjection (at least according to Bede's account), he was chosen to lead the next mission to Northumbria. He would succeed where Corman had failed. The Irishman arrived in Bamburgh in around AD 635 when he founded the monastery on the nearby tidal island of Lindisfarne and became its first bishop. He also established a church and a monastic cell at Bamburgh (almost certainly on the site of the present-day St Aidan's). Bede tells us that he would often stay at Bamburgh, using it as a base to spread the Gospel (*EH* III.17). From here, he travelled tirelessly on foot around Northumbria, preaching to rich and poor (including children and slaves). With support from his patron Oswald, he won many converts by this grounded and no-nonsense approach. In a wonderful historical detail, Bede tells us that the king himself agreed to act as Aidan's interpreter:

"It was indeed a beautiful sight when the bishop was preaching the gospel, to see the king acting as interpreter of the heavenly word for his ealdormen and thegns, for the bishop was not completely at home in the English tongue, while the king had gained a perfect knowledge of Irish during the long period of his exile." (EH III.3)

But just who was Aidan? Bede tells us nothing of his early life in Ireland. To fill in the blanks we must make use of local tradition, and obscure references in saints' calendars – and we must also take the occasional leap of faith, venturing where angels (and academics) fear to tread. Finding the 'real' Aidan, behind the curtain of hagiography, is fraught with perils and pitfalls. The histories are crammed with references to saints and kings called Aidan. Twenty-three holy men of the name are featured in *The Martyrology of Donegal* alone (written by Michael O'Clery in the seventeenth century, but based on earlier evidence). A diminutive of Aodh ('fire'), thought to be a god of the underworld, it crops up as Aodhán, Aidanus, Edanus, Aeddan, Máedóc, Aed, as well as in its more familiar anglicised form, Aidan.

Early on my research for *The Man Who Gave His Horse to a Beggar*, my book following in the footsteps of Aidan, I encountered a saint called Aidan (Máedóc) of Ferns through a holy well, Ffynnon Faiddog [SM 738 427], that bears his name. It can be found just above the beach at Whitesand's Bay near St David's, in Pembrokeshire, South Wales. Born in sixth-century Ireland and active in Britain in the seventh, he founded many monasteries. But this interesting character was not 'our Aidan', and may himself have been a conflation of two men, one Welsh, the other Irish, who served as bishop of Ferns [T 017 498], in modern-day County Wexford, Ireland, a generation apart. Columba was said to have had a nephew called Aidan, but he is too early to be our hero.

The Martyrology of Donegal refers to an *"Aedhan, son of Lughar"* who is *"of the race of Eochaidh Finn Fuath-nairt"*. Aidan's ancestor, Eochaidh Finn, was the grandson of the High King of Ireland, Túathal Techtmar, one of three brothers, including the famous Conn Cétchathach ('of the hundred battles') whose descendants in the Uí Néill and Connachta dynasties dominated Ireland for centuries. Brigit – possibly the famous Saint Brigit of Kildare – was also said to be among Eochaidh Finn's many collateral descendants and, therefore, distantly related to Aidan.

Genealogies like this combine the historical with the legendary, but it is perfectly plausible that Aidan should be related to the warrior kings of prehistoric Ireland. A genetic survey has shown that one in twelve Irish men is descended from a warlord who appears to have been as active sexually as he was militarily, and an estimated three million males worldwide may share this genetic signature. This founder figure has been identified as 'Niall of the Nine Hostages' (though this hypothesis is not without its challengers), from whom St Columba descends and who famously abducted Ireland's Welsh patron saint, Patrick.

Legend has it that Aidan's ancestors, the Fothairt, came to Ireland as mercenaries, with subsequent generations becoming powerful kings and warlords. One theory is that they were part of a larger ethnic group called the Cruthin, an old name for the Britons and the Picts. This idea has assumed a somewhat sinister sectarian dimension in the north of Ireland where it has been used by some Ulster Unionists to show the early presence of 'British' peoples in Ireland. Whatever their origins, the Cruthin were thoroughly absorbed within the Gaelic culture of Ireland and western Scotland. As an ethnic group, they formed a strong component in the kingdom of Dál Riata (this body of water should be seen not as a barrier but rather as a road or bridge, with two-way cultural traffic passing between Britain and Ireland), And it has been suggested that the people of Dál Riata and the Cruthin were two families of the same people, forming a political, cultural and linguistic bridge between the two islands.

Orthodox Christian portraiture shows Aidan as a thin, long-faced man with a bulbous forehead, red forked beard and receding hair, with the hint of a smile hovering on his lips. Such images are not intended to be lifelike portraits but celestial likenesses, a point made by Aidan Hart, a celebrated icon-painter who shares his first name with our hero. It is quite likely that the Irishman was red-haired as his name translates as 'Little Fire'. To this day, Ireland and Scotland have the highest incidences of red hair in Europe. Aidan had strong associations with fire, both in life and in death, and is often shown carrying a torch representing the flame of faith he brought to Northumbria. The saint, despite his reputation for discretion, could be quite outspoken, even curmudgeonly in his dealings with those who fell short of his expectations. And so there emerges another possibility ... that Aidan was a nickname for someone with a fiery temper.

He would have sported a hairstyle known as the 'Celtic tonsure', thought to have been worn by druids as far back as the Iron Age. Experts cannot agree on its exact form, but the head appears to have been shaved in some way from ear to ear. Very different to the Roman 'Friar Tuck' tonsure, instantly recognisable from countless films and television shows from *Cadfael to The Name of the Rose*, it would have lent the monks of Ireland a distinctive, somewhat fearsome appearance.

Aidan would, no doubt, have been lean from walking and fasting, but also muscular from hard work, inured to cold and discomfort, and accustomed through years of austerity to unimaginable hardships. His hands would have been callused, the soles of his feet thickened and cracked at the edges. His breath would have smelled rancid on occasions – fasting is known to cause halitosis – and bathing would have been carried out in cold lakes and sea water not for the purpose of improving personal hygiene but for the mortification of the flesh. If you want to picture the sort of cleric Aidan must have been, forget the clean-shaven vicar and picture instead the hardy pioneer of the Old West, or a member of the SAS. Discipline and self-reliance would have been developed through a life of daily prayer and privation, regulated by strict spiritual leaders, in accordance with the liturgical calendar. *"Let him be steadfast and without a shadow of weakness"* exhorts *The Rule of Ailbe* (a saint who died in the sixth century); *"let him be like an anvil in his support of every profitable thing".*

Aidan almost certainly grew up in a timber home. The practice of building in wood was so characteristic of the Irish or 'Scots' that Bede describes it as *"more Scottorum"*, or *"after the manner of the Scots".* People tended to live in round houses, a style of building that continued from the Bronze Age into the Christian era. Constructed from interwoven saplings known as 'wattle' and plastered with mud and straw called 'daub', their conical roofs were thatched with heather and covered over with mud or turf to keep the heat in and the elements out.

Before Aidan arrived on Iona, he may have been a high-ranking cleric on Scattery Island [SD 914 283] or Inis Chathaigh, in the mouth of the Shannon, in County Clare. Aidan of Lindisfarne is mentioned in several sources, including the ninth-century *Félire Óengusso* ('The Martyrology of Oengus') where he is described as *"Áedán the brilliant sun of Inis Medcoit"* (*"Aedán in grían geldae, Inse Medcoit"*). He appears too in the twelfth-century *Félire Uí Gormáin* ('The Martyrology of Gorman') as *"wise Aidan"* (*"Áedán ergna"*), "bishop of Scattery Island" (*"epscop, o Inis Cathaig"*). We cannot be absolutely sure that this was Aidan of Lindisfarne but the famous Irish priest John Canon O'Halon accepted they were the same person. Intriguingly, saints' calendars link this Aidan not only to Scattery Island but also to Inis Medcoit, the old Celtic name for Lindisfarne.

One possible objection to this identification is that the Aidan mentioned here was apparently already a bishop. Bede, however, claims that he was only raised to this rank when appointed to Lindisfarne. How are we to reconcile these narratives? Reverend Ray Simpson, a leading authority on Aidan, has argued that this apparent contradiction does not necessarily indicate that we are dealing with two different people. The title of bishop was also used in a general sense to refer to the person with oversight, while modern pilgrim networks accept the tradition that there were indeed ancient links between Scattery, Iona and Lindisfarne.

We cannot be sure of the order of business as to when Aidan arrived in Northumbria after a long and arduous journey from Iona. We know he established churches across the kingdom not only at Lindisfarne but also at nearby Bamburgh, on Farne Island and at Old Melrose in the Borders. His arrival heralded an influx of Irish-speakers, including (but probably not limited to) monks from Iona. One of his first jobs would surely have been to oversee the creation of the monastic complex itself, which would have been built largely from timber. The monastery would have served as a hospital, hotel, community centre, prison, market and farm, tending to every need. It would have required not only a church but a library or scriptorium, cells or dormitories for the monks themselves, and a guest house for visitors. It would have needed pens for livestock, vegetable gardens and boats to access the Farne Islands and for fishing.

Because these buildings were almost certainly constructed from perishable materials and were later overlaid by stone structures, little survives above-ground of Aidan's original monastery. However, it was probably in the vicinity of the ruins of the later Norman priory. Somewhere in this area was Aidan's lost school, which must rank among his most significant achievements. Here prayer and study were carried out in earnest in one of the earliest establishments of its kind in Britain. The school counted some of the greatest saints of the age among its students. The boys taught here established monasteries all over Britain including foundations at Lastingham, Hexham and Ripon to name a few. And among the first intake of hugely influential churchmen were Chad (d. AD 672), the Apostle to the Mercians; his brother Cedd (d. AD 664) who evangelised the East Saxons; and Eata (d. AD 686), who went on to become Bishop of Hexham, Abbot of Melrose and Bishop of Bernicia. Perhaps the most influential of all was St Wilfrid (c. AD 633-709) who went on to play such a decisive role in the future of the Church.

A place of great learning and spiritual endeavour, Aidan's school created a production line for saints moulded in the Irish tradition. Here they were taught grammar, mathematics, physics and the classics, as part of a rich and varied education. But the school would have been a great leveller, too, with students drawn from aristocratic backgrounds rubbing shoulders with those whom Aidan had redeemed from slavery:

> "He would never give money to powerful men of the world, but only food on such occasions as he entertained them; on the contrary he distributed gifts of money which he received from the rich, either, as we have said, for the use of the poor or for the redemption of those who had been unjustly sold into slavery. In fact, many of those whom he redeemed for a sum of money he afterwards made his disciples and, when he had trained and instructed them, he ordained them priests." (EH III.5)

On top of the immediate and considerable practical tasks associated with setting up and running a monastery, the overall responsibility for the success of the wider mission also fell to Aidan as bishop. It would be difficult to overstate these challenges. Northumbria was vast: the northernmost portion, Bernicia, roughly equivalent in size to the modern English counties of Northumberland, Durham, parts of Cumbria and the Scottish counties of Berwickshire and East Lothian; the southern portion of Deira, corresponding roughly to the Yorkshire area, extended from the Humber to the Tees, and from the North Sea to the western edge of the Vale of York. This must have presented huge logistical challenges for the Gaelic monks who came here at great personal risk, as well as for the subsequent generation of monks trained under Aidan's direction.

The landscape was more densely-forested than it is today and there was very little the way of infrastructure, with the exception of the overgrown semi-derelict Roman road network. Inland, the kingdom was mountainous, with the Pennines (running north-south) and the Cumbrian fells to the west among the more formidable obstacles. The terrain made east-west movement particularly difficult, restricting overland travel to natural corridors such as the Stainmore Pass on the border of Cumbria, Yorkshire and Durham. This gap in the spine of the Pennines formed part of the Roman road from Scotch Corner to

Penrith, now followed by the modern A66. Another main landward east-west route would have included the old Roman roads alongside Hadrian's Wall, including the Stanegate which connected Carlisle (Luguvalium) and Corbridge (Corstopitum). It is a safe bet that Aidan's paths would have followed similar routes dictated by topography, as they are now.

But unlike today, Britain had a more continental pattern of weather with much colder winters and correspondingly warmer summers. Writing in *An Atlas of Anglo-Saxon England*, David Hill has suggested the land may have been blanketed in snow for an average of 50 days of the year.... yet another impediment to Aidan's efforts to reach isolated communities. The eastern part of the kingdom has a long coastline and several navigable rivers including the Tyne, the Tweed, the Wear and the Tees reaching far inland. The quickest way to get anywhere would have been on horseback or by boat. Aidan, however, usually chose to walk which makes his achievements all the more remarkable. He famously disdained the use of a horse, presenting his steed to the first beggar he met on the road, even though it had been a gift from a king (see page 107).

The landscape was also more dangerous than it is today, inhabited by wolves and wild boar. As late as the eleventh century, a monk named Galfrid observed that wolves were so numerous in Northumbria that it was virtually impossible for even the richest flock-masters to protect their sheep. It would have been difficult to reach some of these isolated settlements and, once there, even more challenging to win the people's trust. The scattered communities of the time would have been wary of strangers, perhaps even downright hostile. This clause from a law code issued early in the reign of King Wihtræd of Kent (AD 695) gives some idea of the sort of welcome travellers arriving unannounced in this period might expect to receive:

> *"If a traveller from afar or a foreigner leave the road, and he then neither shout nor blows a horn, he is to be regarded as a thief, to be either killed or ransomed."*
> from *Anglo-Saxon Prose* (1993), translated by Michael Swanton

Suspicion of outlanders would have been even greater in Northumbria, a kingdom whose population had recently suffered a catalogue of atrocities at the hands of Cadwallon's invading army. According to Bede, the Welsh king has spent a year *"not ruling them like a victorious king but ravaging them like a fearful tyrant, tearing them to pieces with fearful bloodshed" (EH III.1)*. Bede's accounts of the depredations visited upon the Northumbrians here and more generally suggest something more sinister than the reprisals of a victorious warlord, more a systematic campaign of torture and ethnic cleansing:

> *"But Cædwalla, although a Christian by name and profession, was nevertheless a barbarian at heart and disposition and spared neither women nor innocent children. With bestial cruelty he put all to death by torture and for a long time raged through all their land, meaning to wipe out the whole English nation from the land of Britain." (EH II.20).*

And if credence is given to Bede's accounts of the depredations visited upon the people of Northumbria, Aidan's mission was comparable to travelling to the killing fields of Rwanda or Kosovo with a message of good news. One can imagine the reception he might expect to receive from the survivors of rape, torture and genocide, as he spoke to them in broken English of a loving God. It is certainly worth considering how Aidan would have been treated as he greeted the general population in a tongue that was not his own and in which he was not yet fluent.

But while the solitary monk roaming the wilderness armed only with prayer is an appealing idea, Aidan must also have travelled with a team of helpers, as he did when he made the journey from Iona. Oswald's court was peripatetic, and it would have made sense to take advantage of the protection and exposure afforded by travelling with Oswald's retinue as it moved between royal centres. The main ones we know about were at Bamburgh, where the famous Castle now stands, and at Yeavering in the foothills of the Cheviots.

One of his first practical challenges would have been to overcome the language barrier. Aidan spoke Old

St. Oswald Receiving St. Aidan by Ford Madox Brown
© Lady Lever Art Gallery, National Museums Liverpool / Bridgeman Images

Irish but his adoptive people spoke a Germanic language known retrospectively as 'Anglo-Saxon' or 'Old English'. Considerable skill and imagination would have been required to make his message relevant to his adoptive people. This was simultaneously a 'top-down' conversion of the ruling elite, as well as a 'bottom-up' grassroots movement intended to bring as many as possible into the Church. Aidan would have been required to speak to king and to commoner, tailoring his message to both, and invoking their respective frames of reference.

Even with the king's obvious support, he would have understood that his success was by no means guaranteed and that the odds may even have been stacked against him. Corman's failed attempt to convert the pagan Northumbrians would surely have been in his mind. Aidan would also have known that his predecessor's failed endeavour had not been the first Christian mission to the region to hit the buffers. A decade earlier, the Italian bishop Paulinus ventured north with the blessing of Edwin (c. AD 586 – 632/633), Oswald's predecessor and maternal uncle, and baptised many across Northumbria. Even the king himself had shown initial reluctance to adopt the new faith, and only took the plunge after considerable efforts to persuade him. When Edwin was cut down in battle in AD 633, his Christian widow Æthelburh fled back to her father's kingdom in Kent and Paulinus went with her. Given what we know of the campaign of mass-murder that was to follow, it was an eminently sensible move. However, it also meant the mission had collapsed. Any gains for the new faith appear to have been superficial and short-lived, though it is highly likely many of the British peoples living further inland were already Christian.

A measure of Aidan's success is that Christianity survived and thrived under successive kings even after Oswald, Aidan's great patron and benefactor, was himself cut down in battle less than a decade into his reign in the Battle of Maserfield in AD 641 or AD 642. One reason for Aidan's evangelical triumph was his recognition of the importance of high-status women. He encouraged the establishment of mixed sex convents and double monasteries, a revolutionary move at the time. He invited an Irishwoman named Hieu to take vows and establish a small monastic group at Heretu ('island of the hart') – Hartlepool, in modern-day County Durham. She became Northumbria's first holy recluse, and was succeeded by the famous

Hild a year later. One of Britain's greatest female saints, Hild or Hilda was related to the Deiran royal line, and baptised by Paulinus in York under the earlier Roman mission. But she was thoroughly steeped in the traditions of Irish monasticism, and it was Aidan who influenced the course of her career more than anyone else.

Faced with a shortage of homegrown opportunities, she planned to follow her sister and take the veil on the Continent. However, in around AD 647, Aidan called her back and convinced her that her talents would be better employed in the service of her own people. And how much poorer might the history of Britain have been without his intervention? His vision was, in part, a rejection of men-only monasticism in favour of a more inclusive model. Winning high-status female converts and cultivating their friendship was essential to the continuing success of the mission. No trace of this monastery remains today, though the monastic cemetery has been found on the headland near St Hilda's Church [NZ 528 337], the heads of the female skeletons resting on stone pillows. Stones inscribed with runes and crosses bearing the names of the saint's sister and mother have also been found, here. Aidan's move created the beginnings of a dynasty of saintly queens and abbesses. His decision allowed Whitby and its daughter houses to assume a level of prestige comparable to men-only monasteries such as Lindisfarne, empowering a long line of powerful female figures who continued to wield considerable influence after Aidan's death.

Despite his considerable achievements, Aidan has been overshadowed by another northern saint who came later and achieved far less – a man by the name of Cuthbert (c. AD 634 – 687). This celebrated Anglo-Saxon holy man was certainly important, but the growth of his legend has been at the expense of a much greater saint. Visitors to the Holy Island of Lindisfarne would be forgiven for thinking that it was Cuthbert rather than Aidan who founded the first monastery here. One of Britain's most important missionaries – the main architect of the conversion – quickly became a peripheral figure, even in the medieval north where he played such an important role. Saint Cuthbert had usurped Aidan's position as the founding father of Lindisfarne's episcopal dynasty.

Even the countless fossil fragments washed up on the shoreline are 'St Cuddy's beads'. The eider ducks, popularly believed to enjoy his protection, are 'Cuddy ducks', and he has two caves in Northumberland named after him. By contrast, there appears to be just one holy well named after St Aidan of Lindisfarne in the whole of Britain, famous for its cure of skin diseases and asthma. Known also as St Iten's Well [NO 534 641], it is to be found near Kirkton of Menmuir, in Angus, though little more than a rarely-visited trickle now remains. Even this dedication is far from certain. The only ancient church dedicated to Aidan in the whole of the UK and Ireland is at Bamburgh. It is said to mark the place where he died on August 31st AD 651, leaning against a buttress of the original timber building. This pioneer, first bishop of Lindisfarne, had to die to get a church named after him.

A major reason for the rise of Cuthbert's cult was the story of his incorruptibility. The monks were said to have opened his coffin for the first time more than a decade after his death, with the intention of placing his bones in a casket, but were staggered to find his body completely intact. It is difficult to disentangle truth from ecclesiastical spin, but as late as the sixteenth century, there were reports that his body was still relatively fresh. The popular appeal of Cuthbert's legend also derived in no small part from the remarkable story of how the monks of Lindisfarne carted his coffin about for seven years – via Melrose, Ripon and Chester-le-Street to name but a few of its temporary resting places – before receiving intimations that Durham was their divinely-appointed destination. An impressive foundation legend like this would have given his cult in Durham a huge lift, helping to promote a flourishing pilgrim trade.

Cuthbert's popularity may have been a product of the genuine love and respect he commanded from ordinary people, but it is also true to say that this was seized upon by clerics to increase their own wealth, status and power. There were also political reasons that set Cuthbert on a trajectory to ecclesiastical superstardom. He presented a much firmer foundation for the edifice of a saintly cult than Aidan. He was Anglo-Saxon rather than Irish and was a safer bet, particularly with the emergence of a sense of English nationhood. Aidan was also a tainted figure because of his association with 'Celtic' Christianity and being on the losing side at the Synod of Whitby. This saw Aidan and his Irish successors who clung to the old ways regarded almost as heretics by the 'Roman' church. Cuthbert, in contrast, was regarded as completely orthodox.

Even in recent months, I have encountered some resistance in online forums to my efforts to raise Aidan's profile and give due credit to his considerable achievements. Some Anglo-Saxon purists do not want to accept that an Irishman played such a significant role in the cultural identity of an 'English' kingdom. This is why Aidan's story remains relevant today. He personifies a shared heritage that transcends modern notions of Irishness, Scottishness, Englishness, Welshness or Britishness or any other national, regional or religious divisions. He travelled widely within Britain and Ireland, from the Shannon to the Hebrides and across the length and breadth of the vast kingdom of Northumbria, and to places unrecorded, too. This was a pioneer man who crossed mountains, seas and rivers to overcome tribal, religious and linguistic barriers. His very life was lived in defiance of borders, both social and geographical. He was descended from peoples who settled on both sides of the Irish Sea, contributing to the genetic and cultural makeup of Britain, of Ireland and beyond.

This was an Irishman who lived in what would become Scotland and moved to what is now northern England, and all before any of these countries existed. Aidan was an Irish-Scot who devoted his life to all the peoples within his mission area, without discrimination. He would make the perfect saint for our divided times, a rallying point at which to remember what we all share. At a time of profound division and uncertainty in Britain and elsewhere, who better than Aidan to help bring unity and reconciliation than a man renowned for his diplomacy who had connections throughout our troubled lands?

This is one reason why Aidan has been mooted not just as the 'Apostle of the English' (as he was famously described by Bishop of Durham Joseph Lightfoot 1828-1889), but as a patron saint of the United Kingdom. Among those leading the call is the theologian and academic, Dr Ian Bradley, an expert on 'Celtic Christianity'. Efforts have also been made to boost Aidan's profile worldwide, in particular by the International Community of Aidan and Hilda, an ecumenical body founded by Ray Simpson which draws inspiration from the lives of these Celtic saints. What Aidan shows is that Northumbria was enriched not diminished by contact with other cultures. Treasures like the Lindisfarne Gospels and the Book of Kells could not have been produced without contacts forged and nurtured by pioneers like Aidan. The Book of

Durrow is the oldest complete illuminated Gospel book in the 'Insular' world (Britain and Ireland). However, experts cannot decide whether it was made in Ireland, what would become Scotland or what is now north east England. The book remains at the centre of a contest over who has made the greatest contribution to the artistic traditions of the 'British Isles'. But in focussing on claims and counterclaims – which are driven by entirely modern anachronistic questions of national identity and of cultural ownership – we risk missing the obvious point that Ireland and northern Britain, including Northumbria, were then part of a single cultural province.

The eclectic design of the Book of Durrow draws together Anglo-Saxon metalwork motifs, illustrations from Coptic (Egyptian) and Syriac (Syrian) manuscripts, while the depictions of the Jesus and the Evangelists echo the figures carved on Pictish stones. Regardless of where (or when) the manuscript was made, it stands as a testament to a cross-fertilisation, providing evidence of how cooperation, mutual influence and the sharing of ideas led to a remarkable cultural flowering. In Aidan's time, it is also worth remembering that Bamburgh was not a barbarian outpost but a thriving cosmopolitan centre where all these influences coalesced. Interestingly, isotope analysis of the skeletons found in the Bowl Hole cemetery, not far from the Castle, show that Aidan's parishioners came from western Scotland, Ireland, Scandinavia and even from as far afield as North Africa and the southern Mediterranean.

Even behind the curtain of hagiography, one can see that Aidan's life was one of service and of sacrifice. His was an existence characterised by an endless giving of himself to others, and even in death this continued through the division and distribution of his remains. He believed in being kind to the poor, in a simplicity of life, and a respect for all people from slaves to kings, as well as being a great advocate for women. He stood for hard work and gruelling discipline, was a stern taskmaster who made big demands of those who spent time in his company, though like all true leaders he did not ask of them to do anything he was not prepared to do himself. Bede is emphatic on this point:

"Aidan taught the clergy many lessons about the conduct of their lives but above all he left them a most

salutary example of abstinence and self-control; and the best recommendation of his teaching to all was that he taught them no other way of life than that which he himself practised among his fellows. For he neither sought nor cared for worldly possessions but he rejoiced to hand over at once, to any poor man he met, the gifts which he had received from kings or rich men of the world." (EH III.5)

He practised what he preached, spurring others to follow his example when it came to fasting and personal holiness. The life he lived was one of constant activity, be it that of prayer or of learning, of walking incomprehensibly vast distances, and of managing the major players in a cut-throat political climate.

Because Aidan was on the 'wrong side' of the Synod of Whitby, Bede had every reason to underplay Aidan's influence, but he does not. There appears to be genuine affection in his account:

"Such were his love of peace and charity, temperance and humility; his soul which triumphed over anger and greed and at the same time despised pride and vainglory; his industry in carrying out and teaching the divine commandments, his diligence in study and keeping vigil, his authority, such as became a priest, in reproving the proud and mighty, and his tenderness in comforting the weak, in relieving and protecting the poor ... All these things I greatly admire and love in this bishop and I have no doubt that all this was pleasing to God." (EH III. 17).

And there is no doubt that Bede thought of Aidan as a saint worthy of celebration. While he only attributes to the Irishman three main miracles (see pages 104-106), he indicates that there were almost certainly more (*EH* II.15).

Aidan died in the seventeenth year of his episcopate, worn out from his labours and heartbroken following the murder of Oswin, (the same man who had given him the horse). Bede makes a point of mentioning that Aidan died less than a fortnight after his friend had been killed. The Irishman fell ill outside his monastic cell in Bamburgh, thought to be the site of the present village church that still bears

The Death of St. Aidan, sketch for the Church of St. Aidan (litho), by Frank Brangwyn
Private Collection / Liss Fine Art / Bridgeman Images © The Estate of Frank Brangwyn / Bridgeman Images

103

his name. He was said to be leaning against the wooden prop or buttress supporting the building from the outside when he breathed his last. This contact relic is associated with several miracles and is traditionally identified with a y-shaped beam high up on the ceiling of the baptistry in St Aidan's Church. An ornate shrine in the church itself is said to mark the place where Aidan died.

It is more than mere hyperbole to say that, without Aidan, there would be no cult of Saint Cuthbert, for the Irishman established the very culture and institutions that allowed his more famous English successor to rise to prominence. Indeed, it was Cuthbert's famous vision of Aidan's soul being taken up to heaven that was said to have inspired the Northumbrian to take up holy orders in the first place. According to *The Anonymous Life of Cuthbert*, a young man was tending his flocks in the Lammermuir hills overlooking the Leader Water, when he saw angels bearing *"to heaven a holy soul, as if in a globe of fire"*. In his *Life of Saint Cuthbert*, Bede describes a *"stream of light breaking in upon the darkness of the long night"*, and a heavenly host descending to earth to retrieve a *"soul of exceeding brightness"*. But, in an ironic twist, the fire of Cuthbert's fame was to burn much more brightly in the centuries to come, an injustice that I have done my best to remedy.

Aidan's miracles

Endowed with the gift of prophecy, Aidan was said to have foreseen a storm at sea. Ahead of their voyage, he provided a monk on the expedition with holy oil to quell the tempest and avert disaster (*EH* III.15).

On another occasion, Bede reports that Aidan invoked divine aid to protect Bamburgh from attack. Unable to breach the stronghold's defences, the pagan warlord Penda of Mercia razed the wooden buildings round about and heaped a vast bonfire on the landward side of the Castle rock. He, then, waited for a favourable wind before setting it alight in a bid to burn his enemies alive, a spectacle that Aidan witnessed from his island retreat on Inner Farne:

"When he saw the tongues of flame and the smoke being carried by the winds right above the city walls ... he raised his eyes and hands towards heaven and said with tears, 'Oh Lord, see how much evil Penda is doing'. As soon as he uttered these words, the winds veered away from the city and carried the flames in the direction of those who had kindled them, so that, as some of them were hurt and all of them terrified, they ceased to make any further attempt on the city, realising that it was divinely protected." (EH III.16)

This event is why Aidan – alongside the third-century St Florian – is sometimes regarded as the patron saint of firefighters.

But perhaps Aidan's most famous miracle involves his patron, Oswald. The king was seated next to the bishop Aidan at an Easter feast when a silver dish was set before him (EH III.6). Just as the bread was about to be

Reputed to be the beam that St Aidan was leaning on when he died at Bamburgh in AD651. The beam is now located above the baptism font at the rear of the church, under the bell tower.
© John Connell

blessed, signalling the formal start of festivities, a servant appointed to relieve the poor entered the hall and told Oswald that a large crowd of starving men, women and children had gathered outside, begging for alms. Oswald immediately ordered food to be carried out, and the silver dish to be broken up and divided among them. Impressed by this act of piety and compassion, Aidan seized his right arm and declared, *"May this arm never perish"*. The prayer was apparently efficacious, with the limb remaining incorrupt after it was cut from his body in battle.

Aidan continued to work miracles even after his death, thwarting Penda's fire-starting antics for a second time. (*EH* III.17) Bede reports that the pagan king returned to Bamburgh a few years after the saint's death with another army and torched Aidan's wooden church, putting the surrounding village to fire and sword. But the buttress that had supported Aidan in the final moments of his earthly life (he is said to have leant against it when he knew death was near) remained unscathed. According to Bede, it survived a second major fire which saw the replacement building likewise burnt to the ground. Bede reports that the flame was licking through the very nail holes of the buttress ... but remained undamaged. When it was again rebuilt, the buttress was placed inside as a focus for veneration. Pilgrims would take splinters and place them in water to cure sicknesses. A wooden beam with a y-shaped fork at one end is still visible inside the twelfth-century fabric of the church and is traditionally identified with the buttress of legend.

Aidan and the gift horse

Aidan was presented with a splendidly-caparisoned horse by King Oswin, to help him on his journeys through the wilds. Unsurprisingly, the king was not best pleased when he learned what had happened, and confronted Aidan as they were going to dinner. The level of detail in the narrative, including the king's somewhat sulky reaction, gives it the ring of authenticity:

St Aidan giving his horse to a beggar – Stained glass in St John Lee, Acomb
© John Connell

> *"My lord bishop, why did you want to give a beggar the royal horse intended for you? Have we not many less valuable horses or other things which would have been good enough to give to the poor, without letting the beggar have the horse which I had specially chosen for your own use?" The bishop at once replied, "O King, what are you saying? Surely this son of a mare is not dearer to you than that son of God?" (EH III.14)*

After brooding on Aidan's words, Oswin threw himself at the bishop's feet and begged his forgiveness. Later the same evening, Aidan grew sad and began to weep. Asked why, he was said to have replied:

> *"I know that the king will not live long; for I never before saw a humble king. Therefore I think that he will be very soon be snatched from this life; for this nation does not deserve to have such a ruler." (EH III.14)*

107

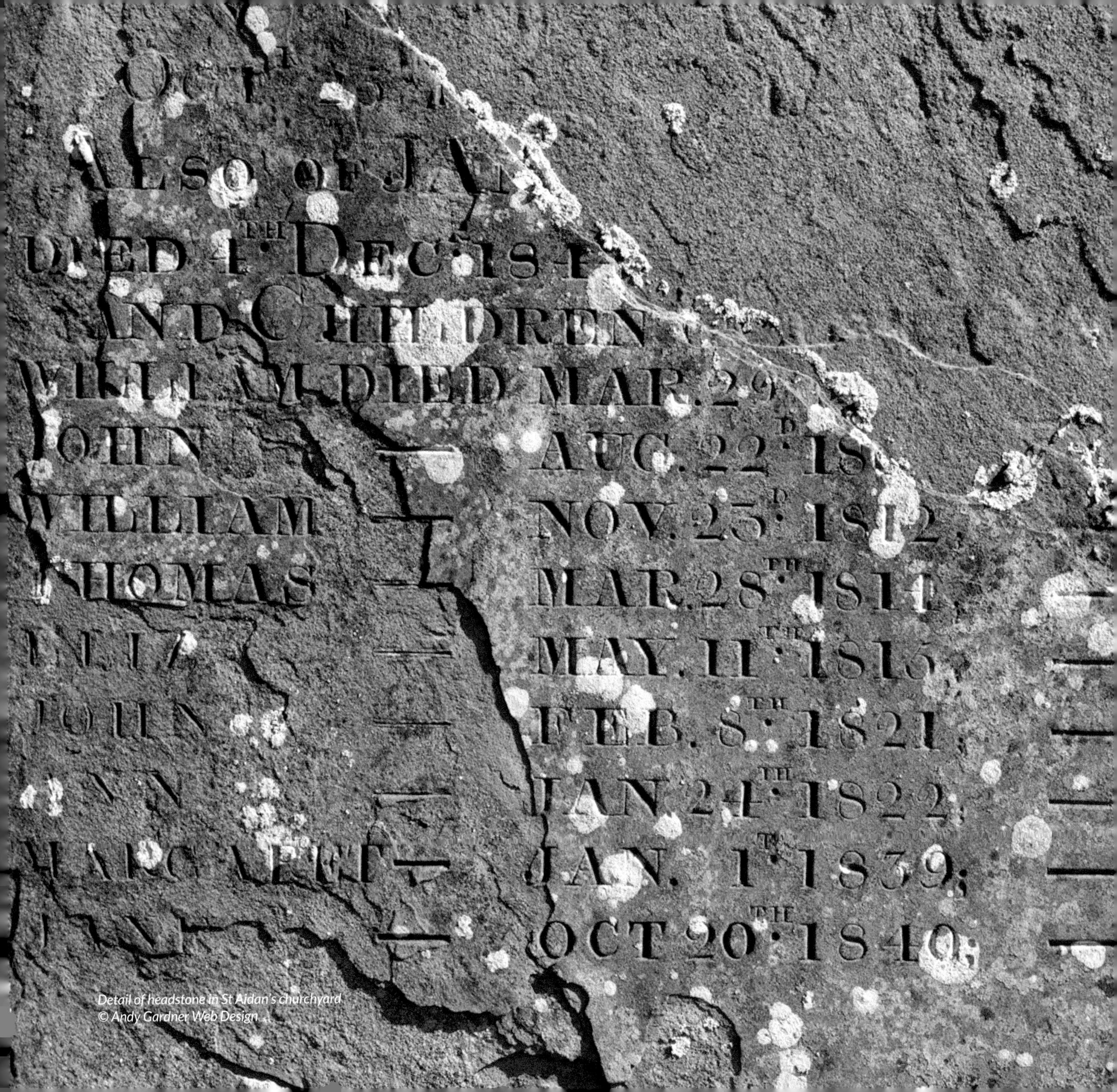

OCT[superscript] ...

ALSO OF JA...

DIED 4TH DEC 184...

AND CHILDREN ...

WILLIAM DIED MAR. 29...

JOHN   AUG. 22D 18...

WILLIAM   NOV. 25D 1812,

THOMAS   MAR. 28 1814,

ELIZ   MAY. 11TH 1815,

JOHN   FEB. 8TH 1821,

ANN   JAN. 24TH 1822,

MARGARET   JAN. 1T 1839,

...   OCT 20TH 1840,

Detail of headstone in St Aidan's churchyard
© Andy Gardner Web Design

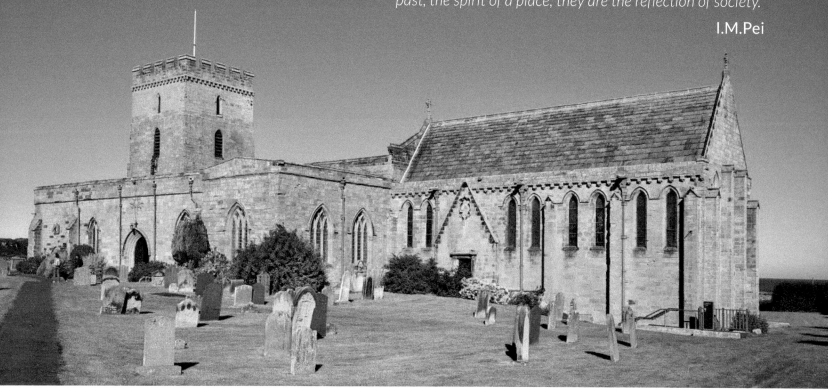

St. Aidan's Church, Bamburgh © R. Mckibbin

St Aidan's Church - An achitectural evolution

Robert McKibbin

Robert McKibbin is a retired architect who is fascinated by the social and cultural stories embodied in our historic buildings. He lives in Northumberland and is an enthusiastic volunteer with Coast Care and the local Wildlife Trust. Most days you will find him investigating rocky headlands or hunting out hill forts in the Cheviots.

Introduction

The words of I.M. Pei could have been written for St Aidan's church alone. The building reflects the resilience of people who suffered centuries of turmoil and deprivation. Their spirit and belief is echoed in each evolution of the church as it grew from a simple wooden structure to the wonderful stone edifice we see today. The story of that building stretches back to the 7th century. As it starts in the fog of the Dark Ages it will be told using what can be seen, what can be pieced together from the historical context and a little bit from what we choose to believe. The wonderful fabric of the church structure and its many beautiful details have already been described by others and so this telling of St Aidan's story focuses on only those major architectural changes that bring the timeline to life.

The First Church

As it stands today St Aidan's consists of a five-bay nave with north and south aisles, a western tower, transepts, and a beautiful chancel with a crypt below its east end.

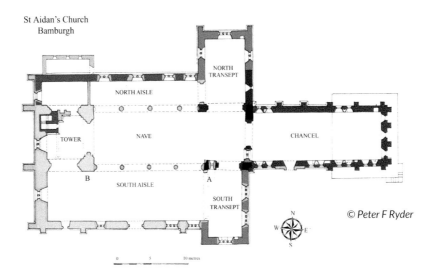

St Aidan's Church
Bamburgh

NORTH TRANSEPT

NORTH AISLE

TOWER

NAVE

CHANCEL

B

A

SOUTH AISLE

SOUTH TRANSEPT

© Peter F Ryder

0   5   10 metres

Teasing open the story of how it evolved from the work of carpenters to the work of master masons is not a simple exercise. Clues are needed and only so many can be extracted from a visual inspection of today's church. The rest must come from a consideration of Saxon and Norman building practices, the mindset of local rulers and the religious and social backdrop that existed in Northumbria as it moved out of a bloody Dark Age battleground.

The story opens in AD 635 with a monk being summoned by a king to create a Christian mission. According to Bede, the great ecclesiastical historian, when Oswald became King of Northumbria he was *"anxious that the whole race under his rule should be filled with the grace of the Christian faith"*. He requested a bishop from the Celtic monastery on Iona and, after a hiccup with the initial choice, Aidan arrived. The king provided Aidan with Lindisfarne as the centre of his mission but they also worked together to build a church close to Oswald's fortress on the Great Whin Sill headland in Bamburgh.

Bede tells us that Aidan had a church and a cell on the royal estate of Bamburgh. It is almost certain that Aidan's first church was a simple building in timber with a thatched roof. No evidence of that 7th century church, or any subsequent timber church, remains today. Aidan died on 31 August 651 under an awning that was attached to the west end of his church. As Bede puts it *"...he breathed his last, leaning against the buttress which supported the church on the outside"*. These details were reported second hand to Bede as he had not been born when Aidan died. The actual buttress must have been pointed out to Bede because he believes it survived two fires before it was set up inside the church, which he also notes was rebuilt twice. The wooden buttress with a forked top, now mounted above the baptistery, is the correct shape to act as a vertical support for a timber roof structure. Whether it is from the original church in unknown. What we do know is that when a large piece of solid oak is subjected to a fire it will char and this action protects it from further damage.

Before considering what a Saxon or Norman church could have looked like if it existed on the site of St Aidan's it is worth summarising the relevant architectural periods the story will move through:

Style	Date	Period
Anglo-Saxon	449 - 1066	5th to 11th century
Norman	1066 - 1189	11th and 12th centuries
Early English	1189 - 1307	13th century

Architectural Styles

The 'Style' names do not designate a precise separation as they are based partly on historical periods and partly on architectural characteristics. The transition date from one style to the other was more gradual than suggested by the precision of the 'Dates' provided and evidence of an earlier period was often absorbed or concealed by works in a later period.

Was there a Saxon church and what could it have looked like?

 The period up to the 11th century was the most tumultuous in Northumberland's history. The ravages of time and raiders from Denmark mean there is little evidence of any pre-Conquest architecture remaining in the church structure. This paucity of information makes it impossible to come to a definitive view on the likely existence of an Anglo-Saxon church. However, it does allow for some judicious conjecture based on an assessment of the anomalies in St Aidan's stonework and a comparison with other known Anglo-Saxon churches built in pre-Conquest Northumbria.

The passage from timber church to stone church would not have been instantaneous. One early form of Saxon church, known as the 'tower-nave', had a tower as its centrepiece with small

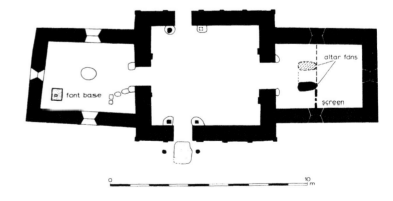

Barton-upon-Humber as it looked in the 10th century

chambers to the east and west. They occur near the coasts of Northumberland, Durham and East Anglia which suggests they were a response to Danish invasions and the tower had a dual purpose as a look-out and as part of the ground floor of the church. A good example of this form is St Peter's church, Barton-upon-Humber.

Is there any evidence that this form of evolution, or something like it, occurred with St Aidan's? There is and it comes from two sources. The first piece of evidence can be gleaned from an interpretation of the floor plan and stonework of St Aidan's and the second from an assessment of what was happening in the surrounding area.

Floorplan and stonework

An inspection of the floor plan at the crossing in St Aidan's shows that some of the walls are skewed slightly to the east away from the line of the nave. Poor setting out of the floor plan was a common defect in Saxon buildings and this specific form of tower/nave misalignment is obvious at Barton-upon-Humber. Other

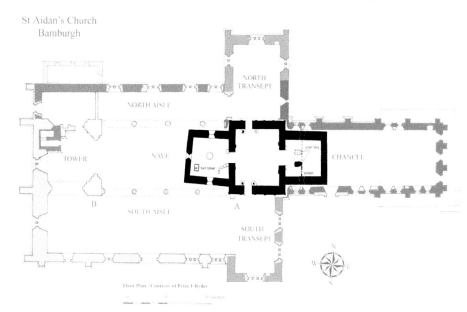

examples exist. The south sides of Brixworth's nave and Earls Barton's tower, both in Northamptonshire, are significantly shorter than the north and the Saxon nave at Chickney in Essex contains not one right-angled corner. By way of comparison the plan of Barton-upon-Humber has been overlaid on St Aidan's floor plan using the skewed St Aidan's wall as a setting out guide.

Possible footprint of the Saxon church based on 11th century stonework

113

There is little physical evidence directly linking the church to the pre-Conquest period. However, a vertical section of the south crossing wall is constructed in rubble with a rough and unworkmanlike appearance.

Rubble walling in the wall between the crossing and the south transept © R. McKibbin

This is typical of Saxon stonework as ashlar was very rarely used for walling. It is likely this rough rubble is the face of the west wall of a narrower transept which was exposed when the later, wider, south transept was built. At 900mm thick it is on the upper end of a typical Saxon wall but this could be explained if it was part of a tower structure.

Other timeline anomalies exist in the stonework of the northern aisle arcade. The section of high level wall facing the aisle is a mixture of coursed elongated blocks, rubble and almost square blocks with a Romanesque appearance. Could part of this wall have been the original north wall of the Saxon nave?

The north aisle arcade, high level wall showing a mixture of coursed elongated blocks, rubble and square blocks.
© R. McKibbin

Saxon buildings in the area

A second source of evidence comes from what was being constructed in the surrounding areas, especially if they have a relationship to Aidan. Lindisfarne is the spiritual home of Aidan. In 2016 and 2017 excavations in an area known as Heugh Hill revealed the outline of a stone structure comprising a large western chamber and much shorter and narrower eastern chamber. The plan form, stonework and alignment of the rooms suggests that it is a church of early origin and most likely no later than 1050. Only a short distance to the north-west is the Church of St. Mary the Virgin. This has stonework work from the Saxon period, most obviously in the remains of the Saxon arch in the wall dividing the nave from the chancel.

Aerial photograph looking north across Holy Island. The recently excavated foundations of a chapel on the Heugh show to the right of the image in the foreground with St Mary's Church and the Priory in the mid ground to the left of the image.
© R. Carlton

It is clear that in this part of St Aidan's story the church is reticent about giving up its secrets. The echo of the past teases us with the potential of a late Saxon building, possibly a tower-nave church. This leaves an unanswered question, are the remnants of the old rubble stonework shown in the above photo part of a reworked enlargement carried out in the pre-Conquest period or are they Norman?

The Norman church

As we follow the timeline of the story into the 12th century the story told by the church is based more on what we see than what we need to deduce although a little more detective work is required to get us through the quirks of the Norman period.

Round headed window – a possible remnant of the Saxon fabric
© R. McKibbin

After the Norman Conquest there was a spurt of church building. The central tower became a common feature of cruciform structures and also for churches without transepts. In the latter form the interior is divided into three parts. The choir or chancel are located under the tower with the nave to the west and sanctuary to the east. Returning to the interior stonework visible in St Aidan's it is fair to say that if the evidence is weak for the existence of a Saxon church then it is much stronger when the case is made for a Norman structure. The History of Northumberland boldly states: "It appears that there was a complete church in the Norman period, comprising a nave, almost certainly aisleless, north and south transepts, and a chancel, with possibly a central tower". In addition to the south crossing wall the same source identifies the southern part of the east wall of the north transept, with an original round-headed window as Norman features.

The north wall of the nave contains several phases of masonry which suggests it was a pre-existing wall. Considering that a longer nave was favoured by the Normans as a way of forming the typical cruciform shape, it is possible parts of it date from that period. It is not parallel to the south side of the older crossing which means the Norman builders overcame the difficulty of the skewed crossing tower by aligning the north wall of the crossing and the north wall of the nave.

The width of the Norman chancel was narrower than the chancel that exists today. The old width can be deduced by looking at the chancel arch from the east. The impost mouldings either side of this arch extend

117

only part of the way towards the north and south walls of the chancel. On the reverse side of this wall the mouldings extend the full width. It is likely that the ends of the mouldings define the position of the earlier walls. This view is supported by the existence of a break in coursing between the stonework forming the north jamb of the arch, and the adjacent masonry. The length of the Norman chancel cannot be determined with any accuracy. A reasonable assumption would be that it was about one third the length of the new chancel as the slope of the ground to the east increases significantly after that point.

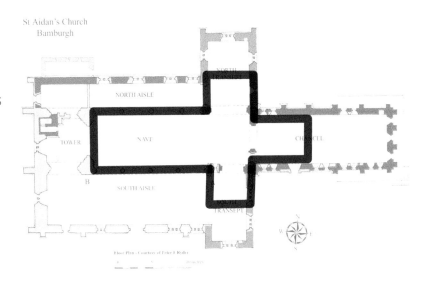

Figure 3: Likely footprint of the Norman Church

Chancel Arch viewed from within the chancel showing the shortened impost mouldings
© R. Turner

Chancel Arch viewed from the body of the church showing the full extent of the impost mouldings
© R. Mckibbin

The Norman church becomes the Early English church we see today?

The story of St Aidan's church and Bamburgh castle become entwined at this point. In 1095, the castle was under the control of Robert de Mowbray but he picked the wrong side in a rebellion against William the Conqueror. He lost everything and the castle was forfeited to the crown. This was bad for Mowbray but ultimately good for Bamburgh as in 1131, under the reign of Henry I, rebuilding of the castle began. Today the main structure

View of St. Aidan's Church looking east, showing the castle in the background illustrated the close physical relationship between the two buildings. © R. Turner

is the great tower which was started in 1164 and completed in 1170 during the reign of Henry II. In 1221, under Henry III, the King's Hall was constructed on the south of the inner ward.

Perhaps it was the security provided by the castle, or a century of relative peace between England and Scotland in the years before 1296, that facilitated the growth of available arable land in Northumberland during the 12th and 13th centuries. Arable areas around Bamburgh were expanding with survey records of 1250 showing that North Sunderland alone had broken in 312 acres of new land. The local population was growing and ultimately there was a need for a larger church.

The end of the 12th century saw the start of a series of additions and remodelling of St Aidan's church. Some researchers have suggested this followed the collapse of a central tower. Phase 1 of this work was an enlargement of the north transept and a northern aisle was formed by inserting an arcade of four bays into the existing north wall of the nave. The easternmost bay is narrower than the other three. The History of Northumberland states this anomaly was probably due to the requirements of ritual but it is possible it was introduced to deal with the old skewed walls being incorporated into the crossing, which was also the location of the old tower. To connect the northern aisle into the main body of the church arches were also formed between the aisle and northern transept and between the transept and the crossing.

It appears that the other arches between the crossing and adjacent areas, including the south transept and chancel were also formed at this time. It is unclear why this was done because no alteration or expansion work was carried out to these areas for some time. The reason may be linked to the Canons of Nostell, a set of Augustine monks. In 1121 they were given the church by Henry I but only after the incumbent priest had died. This happened in 1171 when Henry II was king but he procrastinated as did two subsequent kings and the handover did not formally occur until 1228 when Henry III agreed that Nostell could finally take possession of the church.

The early years of the 13th century saw Phase 2 of the expansion works and the construction of the south aisle. It opened into the nave through an arcade of four bays of equal width and height.

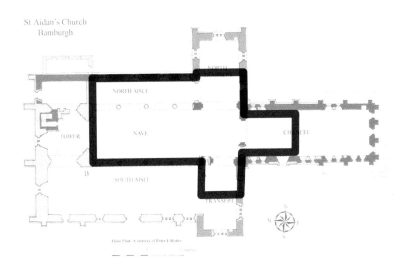

Layout at c1200 church - Phase 1

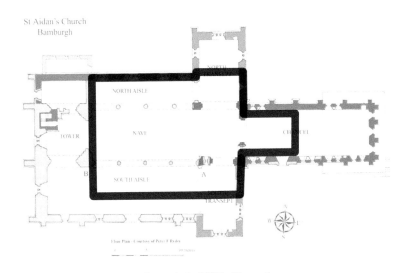

Layout at c1200 - Phase 2

The consensus is that the west tower was built a short time after the expansion of the south aisle even though the architectural features are different. Both the north and south aisles were then extended westwards to overlap the tower, which gains access into the nave and these western extensions through arches which broadly match those in the aisle arcades. This completed Phase 3 of the expansion work to the church.

In 1230 the aspirations of the Canons of Nostell came to fruition and they commissioned the construction of a new chancel which is, without doubt, the most significant alteration carried out to the church. It is unusually long at almost 18 metres and over 6 metres wide. The form of the original roof is unknown and it was not until the end of the 19th century that a pitched roof was erected that complimented the elegance and height of the chancel space. Taking advantage of a sloping site the Nostell builders formed a basement crypt under the east end of the chancel. The crypt is now open to the public and has a fascinating story of its own to tell.

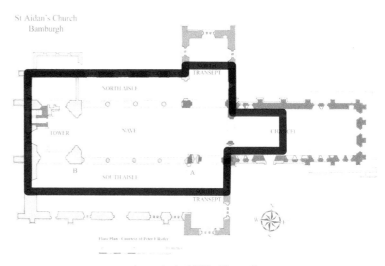

Layout at c1200 - Phase 3

St Aidan's Chancel
© R. McKibbin

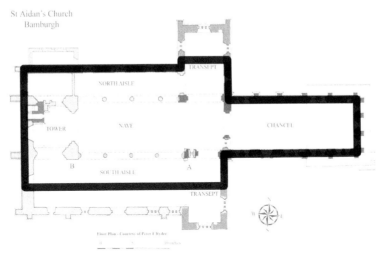

Layout at 1230 with new Chancel and crypt

How did St Aidan's survive the 14th century?

The first half of the 14th century included some of Northumberland's darkest hours. In April 1296 bubbling tensions between the English and Scots resulted in an invasion of Scotland by Edward I. Mixed loyalties and a cross border matrix of land ownership meant that the incursions and battles that followed in a spiral of revenge resolved nothing. In particular Robert Bruce's campaigns struck at the heart of Northumberland and reduced this relatively vibrant area to the point where 200 townships lay deserted by 1327.

During this period of danger and uncertainty floods and bad weather caused a series of poor harvests. The impact was made worse by the spread of sheep and cattle diseases which killed many of the plough oxen. To top it all off in 1348 the Black Death arrived in England and caused a dramatic decrease in the number of people who could work the land. The population in Northumberland reduced from 148,084 in 1290 to 30,389 in 1377.

What happened to St Aidan's during this period? Again being located near the castle and the physical protection that provided was advantageous to the church. Other than a fire which occurred in the first decade of the 14th century there is no other record of damage caused by the Scots or other marauders.

Somehow building work continued as the southern aisle was widened in the first half of the century and the junction with the south transept was increased to form the very wide arch visible today.

The new south elevation now contained two doorways. The larger more ornate of the two originally had a porch attached and it is believed this was for the use of the parish. The smaller door to the west could then have been used by the canons to gain access to the nave for processional purposes without interference from the parochial part of the church.

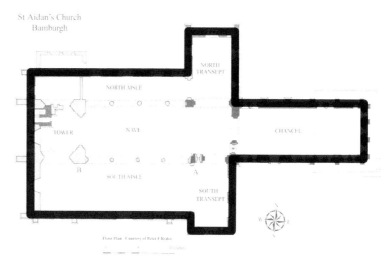

Layout in 14th century with enlarged south aisle

At the same time as the southern aisle was widened, the north and south transepts were lengthened. These works were most likely carried out to accommodate chantry chapels following a number of bequests. The most notable were from William Galoun in 1316 and Thomas de Bamburgh in 1333.

Death and resurrection

The social and economic devastation caused by the Black Death combined with the impact of the Hundred Years War between England and France encouraged the Peasants Revolt of 1381 which ultimately changed the face of the countryside. The English agricultural economy entered a great slump and remained depressed throughout the 15th century. Attempts to rebuild around Bamburgh were not helped when it became embroiled in the War of the Roses between the houses of Lancaster and York. The castle was badly damaged by artillery during a nine month siege in 1464. That was the beginning of a long slow decline and it fell into ruin in the 16th century.

A snapshot of the general state of Northumberland at that time is provided by the future Pope, Aeneas Sylvius Piccolomini, who was on a diplomatic mission to James I of Scotland in 1435. Forced to travel south overland through Northumberland he commented that reaching Newcastle was like entering a habitable country because *"...Scotland and the part of England nearest it are utterly unlike the country we inhabit, being rude, uncultivated, and unvisited by the winter sun."*

It's not surprising that little work was carried out to St Aidan's in this period. The north isle was rebuilt on its old foundations or refaced in the late 15th or early 16th century. Around the same time the square stair was added to the west tower. The use of multiple quarter landings in the stair is unusual and it has been suggested that this indicates the tower was being utilised as a refuge, perhaps from Border reivers who may have seen the declining protection provided by Bamburgh castle as an opportunity. These were the last major works to the church until the end of the 19th century because, like the castle, ruin was soon to befall St Aidan's but for a completely different reason.

In 1536 Henry VIII began the dissolution of the monasteries. The Bamburgh cell was sold to Sir John

Image extracted from the Architectural Survey of 1870 showing the raised gables

Forster for the princely sum of £664 and immediately neglected by him. In 1617 it was recorded that the

"...steeple was only half covered with lead and the other half utterly decayed and open. The church was thatched and indecently kept and defiled with doves. The windows thereof not sufficiently glassed...". Viewed from London, the Stuart elite thought Northumberland was one of the 'dark corners of the land' and a place where the light of southern Protestantism and civility still struggled to penetrate.

St Aidan's did have some vestige of life in the 17th century. *The Architectural Survey of the Churches in the Archdeaconry of Lindisfarne* records that the church register commenced in 1653. This was "*36 years after the church was deformed with doves*" and two years after the end of the English Civil War. It is clear that the core of this resilient parish was making some attempt to maintain the church in a functional state.

The Sharp Memorial located at the west end of the north aisle
© R. Turner

In the 18th century Bamburgh was, for once, struck by good fortune. It came into the ownership of Lord Nathaniel Crewe, Bishop of Durham, and it was favoured by his trust which was set up in 1721. St Aidan's was doubly lucky as Dr John Sharp, Archdeacon of Northumberland, became a trustee in 1758 and for the next three decades further funds were allocated for restoration work. The west end of the north aisle houses a monument given by Catherine Sharp in 1839 as a memorial to her husband and several members of the Sharp family.

In 1870 the state of the church was described as 'excellent' by the Architectural Survey thanks to funds from Lord Crewe's trust. The roof had been renewed, the walls scraped free of plaster and whitewashed, the gables had been raised at the east end of nave and chancel "*ready to receive high pitched roofs at a convenient opportunity*".

Rainwater hopper heads located around the parapet of the chancel are dated 1830. This fixes the timing of a programme of major works that included repairs and refacing of the older stonework. The porch for the priest's door was removed although the historical shadow of that structure can be seen in a rather jarring shallow gabled projection of grey ashlar. In July 1837 the crypt was 'rediscovered'. How it was lost is a mystery as it must have been evident from the outside that there was a basement structure under the chancel. Records would also have shown that the crypt had been used as a burial chamber by the Augustinian canons and the Forster family.

Rainwater hopper dated 1830 © R. Turner

This programme of work also included the re-facing of the whole west end of the church inside and out and a new section was added to the top of the tower. In 1847 the windows in the north and south walls of the chancel were glazed with glass from the Netherlands. In 1857 the nave was re-roofed but it was not until 1895 that work commenced on providing a pitched roof above the chancel running between the two gable ends that had

Grey ashlar projection around the chancel door © R. Turner

been freestanding for at least 25 years. The new roof allowed the lancet windows in the east wall of the chancel to be extended to their original height. The St Aidan's that entered the 20th century is the one that is open for us all to see today.

"Architecture is the very mirror of life"

The architecture of St Aidan's contains physical links back to the 11th century but the church has spiritual links all the way back to Aidan's wooden church erected in the 7th century. The first church reflects the wishes of two men and their desire to bring Christianity to Northumbria. The many different forms it took as the centuries rolled over it mirrored the social and cultural needs of the population of Bamburgh and the surrounding parishes. The church tells a story that reflects the hardships inflicted on the area and the resilience of the people who came to worship in it. St Aidan's church, in all its many forms, truly is the mirror of life.

The Bamburgh Knight

One of the loveliest aspects of the church is the stunning Chancel, complete with the squint (otherwise known as a hagioscope) at the west end, St Aidan shrine, the tall lancet windows of stunningly coloured glass and, at the east end, the reredos depicting the Northern Saints. In a low recess in the south wall quietly lies the figure of a recumbent knight - to be placed in such a prestigious location in the Chancel suggests a figure of some importance but who was he? This mystery has become something of a pre-occupation for amateur historian and former Archdeacon of Northumberland, the Ven. Peter Elliott who has produced a beautiful booklet about the Knight which is available for sale in the church. Evidently the mystery continues to pique Peter's interest and his diligent research has led him away from Bamburgh - making connections to land endowments, political intrigue, ecclesiastical courts in Rothbury, letters from Popes and Kings, the building of Dunstanburgh Castle, Merton College in Oxford and to Thomas Dughan - the last Rector of Embleton – who was also known as Thomas de Bamburgh. A local man of significant standing, connections and affluence to merit a knights effigy in St Aidan's church? As Peter continues on his endeavour to discover all there is to know about the Bamburgh Knight the links between ecclesiastical houses of Bamburgh and Embleton become stronger - hopefully a booklet revision will follow.

The Crypt of St. Aidans

There are many fascinating aspects to St Aidan's church; spiritual, cultural and architectural. One unique attraction is the crypt which lies below the two easternmost bays of the chancel. It was built in 1230 and is an atmospheric space that displays the skills of the medieval stone mason and also provides an astounding link to our very distant past.

On entering the church grounds the entrance to the crypt is concealed from view. Moving closer to the south wall of the chancel reveals a sunken passage. Looking into this passage reveals the footings of the chancel wall piers and also a square-headed doorway. This opening was formed when the chancel was constructed although only the lower section has the original stone surround. Stepping over the threshold a new viewing platform that will transport the visitor from the 21st century back to the 13th century and beyond.

On plan, the crypt is almost square but this is not immediately apparent due to a dividing wall running along the east/west axis which divides it into two unequal parts.

Both parts are of great interest for completely different reasons. The larger southern chamber has an unusual vaulted ceiling above your head and bodies below. The northern chamber, which can glimpsed through a small opening in the dividing wall opposite the entrance steps, is now the final resting place of the Bowl Hole skeletons who lived in Bamburgh 1,400 years ago.

128

Southern chamber

The vaulted ceiling in the southern chamber is formed in two bays. One way to visualise this part of the crypt is to imagine standing in the centre of the stone floor. Directly above, running between the north and south walls is a semi-circular transverse stone rib. Where it meets the walls it is supported on a simple stone corbel. This central arch is common to both vaulted bays.

From the same position, looking towards the east wall, there are two lancet windows. On the left and right ends of this wall there are another two stone corbels about chest height. Springing from each is a diagonal stone rib. As these ribs arc up they cross at the mid-point of the vault and then continue until they land on the same corbels that support the transverse rib.

There is one further addition to the crypt vaults which makes them rather unusual. Normally there would be four panels formed by the transverse and diagonal ribs but here there are five. This is achieved by the addition of a further axial stone rib running from a corbel located between the two lancet windows to the crossing point of the diagonal arches. It isn't clear why this rib was introduced but it does provide space for an aesthetically pleasing pointed arch framing above the head of the windows.

The infill panels between the ribs are formed from individual stones. How do they stay in place? Medieval

Detail of a stone corbel in the crypt
© Andy Gardner Web Design

Two lancet windows in the east wall
© I. Glendinning

stone masons did not have the convenience of modern building methods we take for granted, such as reinforced concrete. Instead, they relied on a deep understanding of geometry and the transfer of structural loads from one element to another using the sequence of construction to ensure stability. Even with no apparent support, the stone infill will not fall on your head.

In addition to the two lancet windows in the east wall there is one in the south wall. They all have a triple step to the internal sill but only the eastern pair have attractive shouldered arches starting, rather unusually, two-thirds up the jamb rather than directly below the lintel.

Beneath the lancet window in the south wall is a piscina, with a small trefoiled arch and a moulded bowl.

A piscina was usually placed near an altar so that liquids from any religious ritual could be disposed of in an appropriate way.

There are other less obvious features in the south chamber. Why are there three small rectangular recesses in the north wall, two in the western bay and one in the eastern? One interpretation is that they supported timber trestles when the space was used as a family burial crypt. Directly above the easternmost recess is a block with a pattern of radial lines. Is this some form of mass dial and if it is, why is it inside where no form of direct sunlight can reach it? If you search the other walls you will find further marks and crosses. They could be symbols or medieval graffiti.

Ribs and infill © Andy Gardner Web Design

Piscina © R. Turner

Possible Mass Clock engraved on the north wall © R. Turner

Northern chamber

Today, access to the northern chamber is provided through the west end of the dividing wall, opposite the main doorway into the crypt. Here there is a small opening about one third the height of a normal door. The size and form of the old stone sill suggests that at one time the opening was even narrower.

This restricted access was not the only way to enter this part of the crypt. There is evidence that one, and perhaps two, other entrances to the north chamber existed. In 1837, as part of the inspection of the 'Death House' as it was known, the floor of the chancel was opened to reveal a flight of stone steps leading through the original wall of the crypt to the northern chamber. Intriguingly the inspection report also records that probings under and near the east window: "...seem to favour the tradition current at Bamburgh that there was a subterranean passage from the religious house directly opposite to the east end of the chancel".

Once inside the northern chamber of the crypt there are two very obvious architectural features: the barrel vault roof and the single lancet window. The vault runs the full length of the chamber. It is built with rough stone and springs from a continuous chamfered moulding running along both long walls. We know from the 1837 inspection that the stone vault was finished with plaster. The single lancet window is similar to those in the east wall of the southern chamber but has a simpler lintel and surround.

The floor is only compacted earth but what stands on it gives this space a poignant spiritual quality. A simple metal frame holds 110 zinc ossuary boxes. Each one contains the bones of an early Christian, exhumed from the nearby Bowl Hole cemetery. Radiocarbon and artifactual dating place the cemetery in the mid-7th to early 9th centuries.

The original purpose of most crypts built in the 13th century was to provide safe storage for ancient relics and a suitable place for their presentation. Today the crypt of St Aidan's protects something equally precious and in doing so completes a religious circle. It is astonishing to think that some of the people whose remains lie in the northern chamber may have actually listened to St Aidan before he died in AD 651 or attended services in the original wooden church, which was built in AD 635 on the very spot where they now rest.

12th century grave marker – in the shape of a roof, with bracelet cross and shears © R. Turner

The Forster Family Vault
Carol Griffiths – project researcher and archivist

By the late 1600s the crypt was being used as the private Forster Family vault. Inlaid into the floor at the east end of the main chamber are five beautiful and simply engraved grave slabs dedicated to members of the Forster Family but this was evidently not how the vault was originally laid out.

The Lord Crewe Collection, held at the Northumberland County Archive at Woodhorn, contains papers covering the 1700s and later, with a huge batch reflecting life in 18th century Bamburgh. One of the most fascinating documents is a very fragile paper dated 1837 recounting the re-discovery of the ancient crypt, when workmen accidentally broke through the floor of the Chancel above and the crumbling coffins of 5 of the famous Forster were exposed. It was to Claudius Forster that King James I had given the ruined Castle in 1610, and it was thanks to the devoted husband of Dorothy Forster, the Aunt of two of occupants of the silent coffins -Thomas and his sister (another) Dorothy - that the Castle had been restored. On the death of Aunt Dorothy's husband Nathaniel, Lord Crewe in 1721 he left his fortune for his late wife's family for the restoration of the castle.

1837– The entrance to the Crypt accidentally rediscovered

Tuesday July 25th 1837 Examined the vaults beneath Bamburgh chancel, Sometimes called the Death House and sometimes the vault of the Forsters.

The oak planks which supported the floor (above) were entirely decayed, and on their removal, there appeared a flight of stone steps leading to the apartments below on examination this was found to pass through the original wall of the vaults, and to terminate in a long arched chamber, like a passage of worked stone, the arch having been finished with plaster, resting on a cornice, and with a narrow window at the east end

The different probings of the floor seem to favour the tradition current in Bamburgh, that there was a subterranean passage from the religious house directly opposite to the east end of the chancel

At the foot of the steps was a square opening into a second apartment, the sides of which had been rudely broken, and which seemed to be a doorway

This second apartment was a highly finished chamber with a groined stone roof, and the east end, on a rude stone platform, were laid five coffins, resting from North to South, a space of about 2 1/2 ft being left open between the platform and the south wall.

In the south wall was a receptacle for Holy Water, and above this a narrow window. At the East end are two windows of the same character, and on the south side a large doorway, traces of which appear on the outer walls of the chancel.

In the roof is an iron staple, probably for suspending a lamp.

This apartment has undoubtedly been a Chapel. But what has been the purpose of the long-passage-like apartment to the North, running parallel to it, East and West?

My conjecture is, that the dead of the adjoining religious house, of which the chancel is supposed to be a remaining part, were laid here previous to interment, for the religious ceremonies then used; and perhaps the dying were brought here for extreme unction

Probably these apartments were afterwards employed as a bone-house and then shut up, and made the vault of the Forster family. They occupy the breadth of the chancel from the first stone eastwards. They are airy and dry.

Therein were five Coffins, resting on a rude stone platform at the east end of the Chapel-

First Mr B Forster of Adderston d. 1765-the body of John or William had been moved to make way for this coffin

Secondly Fernando Forster d. 1701 said to have been murdered by Frederick of Bywell

Thirdly John or William Forster

Fourthly General Forster whose body was brought from France in 1738. Privately buried being brought in a hearse with one horse and a single servant attending

Fifth-Dorothy Forster d. 1739 Married Armstrong afterwards of the Friars - an inferior person

The first coffin was perfect [containing Mr. Bacon Forster, nephew of General Tom]

The second of wood only [containing the body of the murdered Ferdinando] had fallen to pieces, but there was the trace of a whole figure, the legs and thigh bones entire, and in place of the skull, on which the coffin lid had fallen, was a mass of white dust like lime

The third, [containing the body of Ferdinando's brother John or William] in much the same state but here the skull of the figure had not crumbled to dust

The fourth [containing the body of General Tom] was perfect except only the cloth covering The outer coffin, of elm, was entire and strong.

It was said that 30 years ago, an opening had been made near the foot to ascertain the presence of the body, which had been disputed. It rested in sawdust closely packed; the Linen clothes were there, and the leg fleshy and perfect. No further examination was at that time permitted.

Mr. Embleton thought he detected the smell of hartshorn near this coffin"

The fifth [containing the body of Dorothy, sister of General Tom] was in a disgusting state, the coffin having fallen to pieces, but the remains not being consumed.

The ribbon which had confined the jaw of the corpse was lying near it.

These coffins had been exposed throughout to the action of air; in decency and prudence they should be buried where they lie

A coffin filled with sawdust only was a few years since, dug up in the Chancel, never having had a body in it, which strengthened the suspicion that General Forster's body was not in the vault

This General Forster was delivered from prison being condemned to death, by his sister Dorothy, now lying by his side. She rode to London on a double horse behind the Adderstone Blacksmith in the quality of a servant and procuring an impression of the prison key, liberated her brother, remaining in his place.

The Smith's name was Purdy, and his descendants of that name are blacksmiths at Adderstone to this day.

Lord Crewe was present at the removal of the family pictures from the Old Hall, once the religious house, now Mr. Grey's farmstead. Barty Younghusband's Father made the cases and had the Bishop's Blessing

C.T [Charles Thorp]
Bamburgh Castle
September 1837

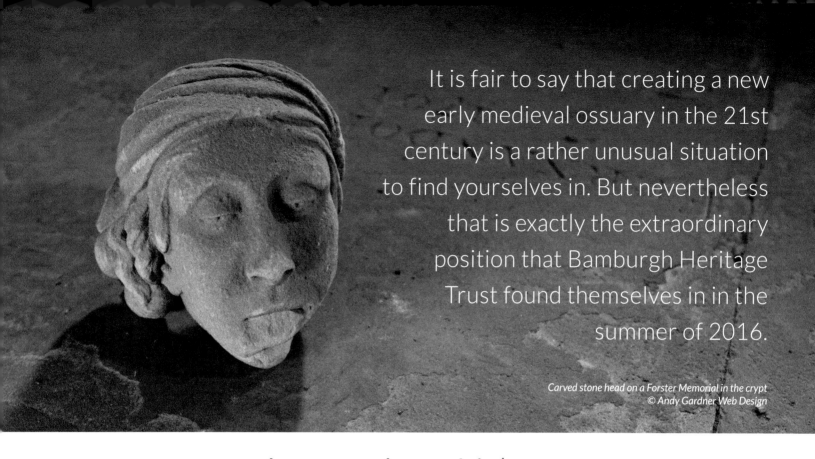

It is fair to say that creating a new early medieval ossuary in the 21st century is a rather unusual situation to find yourselves in. But nevertheless that is exactly the extraordinary position that Bamburgh Heritage Trust found themselves in in the summer of 2016.

Carved stone head on a Forster Memorial in the crypt
© Andy Gardner Web Design

Accessing Aidan

Jessica Turner

The story starts a little early in 2012 when a fantastic Bamburgh lady called Jude Aldred became the driving force behind the newly created small local heritage group – Bamburgh Heritage Trust (BHT). There is no doubt that Bamburgh has an incredibly rich heritage offer, from the beautiful fabric and grain of the village itself to the incredibly imposing castle perched upon the dominant dolerite rock to the close association to the Victorian heroine Grace Darling. Grace's story is beautifully told at the dedicated RLNI museum located on Radcliffe Road and the castle appropriately celebrates the great Victorian industrialist Lord Armstong and his family. So, the ambition of Bamburgh Heritage Trust was to try and tell some of the other stories –

like the stories of the village's sacrifices during two world wars, the story of border war strife, Dr. Sharp's social reform, the resident suffragette firebrand Nora Balls, the colourful stories of the Forster dynasty and the most astounding of all – Bamburgh's central importance in our nation's Anglo-Saxon history.

Graeme Young's chapter illustrates the political and religious significance of Bamburgh in the early Anglo-Saxon period as the pre-eminent royal palace site at the time of King Oswald and how the Bowl Hole cemetery dates from around AD 650 – a period of relatively stability and prosperity for the Northumbrian kingdom and the establishment of the Celtic Christian religion through the influence of the gentle St Aidan.

Matthew 24:27 (NKJ):
"For as the lightning comes from the east and flashes to the west, so also will the coming of the Son of Man be . . .
. . . Priest/bishops other way round to see the flock but also same position as when in church"

The skeletons excavated from the Bowl Hole cemetery were all roughly in an east-west alignment and this coupled with very few grave goods immediately suggested to archaeologists that they were dealing with a Christain burial ground. The few grave goods that were uncovered were very much of a domestic nature such as pins, buckles and small knives but also suggested an Anglo-Saxon date. The discovery of the cemetery site was remarkable but the

Carved stone head on a Forester Memorial in the crypt © Andy Gardner Web Design

good level of preservation and the importance of Bamburgh at the time this community were living made this a nationally significant find. The subsequent osteological analysis done by Prof Charlotte Roberts and Durham University added a fascinating insight into the health, disease and diet of our Anglo-Saxon ancestors. And the isotope analysis of the teeth enamel of every skeleton painted an even more fascinating picture - of a cosmopolitan population living in Bamburgh 1,400 years ago. Less than 10% of the skeletons excavated from the cemetery site originate from Bamburgh. With others coming from the West of Scotland, Ireland, Cumbria and continental Europe including Scandinavia and much further south possibly Italy and Spain. Whilst it is not possible to know the reasons for this migration – it could have been socio-economic, religious, political, trade, anything – we can appreciate that travel 1,400 years ago across countries and continents would have been a remarkable and arduous undertaking. It demonstrates extraordinary endeavour and just like us, these people lived and worked in this spectacular coastal village or travelled from far and wide to visit and enjoy its treasures.

The location of the cemetery site, so close to the castle, immediately suggest a close association with the castle. If nothing else digging grave cuts in the dolerite rock of the castle's rocky outcrop would have been neither practical or desired so the site to the south of the castle is actually the nearest feasible workable earth surface as well as having the capacity to hold a large number of inhumations. The location also reflects the prevailing Roman tradition of burials along the major routes out of the settlement and the law forbidding burial within town walls. The move to Christain burials in consecrated burial grounds became more commonplace from about 800AD onwards after Cuthbert, the then Archbishop of Canterbury obtained papal permission in 752 to set up of churchyards within cities and a 10th century copy of the Pontifical of Egbert, Archbishop of York (732–766) sets out the rituals for the consecration of a cemetery and this suggests that this practice was happening during and subsequent to Egbert's time. The start of the Bowl Hole cemetery predates the move to consecrated ground and we have evidence for a church within the castle so it is reasonable to assume that the Bowl Hole continued as the burial ground for castle residents and that 'villagers' focus would have been around the church founded by St Aidan in 634, on the site of today's church.

The relatively good preservation of the skeletal remains, coupled with the extensive archaeological investigation of the cemetery site and the castle site together with extraordinary osteological research means we know a remarkable amount about this congregation – generally, the population was robust, tall and healthy apart from the terrible dental hygiene, this is all indicative of a good diet. We know where they came from, we know they were linked to the Royal court, we know their aliments, their aches and pains and their age. We can go a little further and speculate what some of these people did for a living, the wear and tear of a life of physical work shows

The chancel of St Aidan's Church
© J Turner

on their bones like the Irish lady with evidence of a condition called Ischial bursitis - more colloquially known as Weaver's Bottom which is linked to repetitive crouching and sitting on a hard surface and this coupled with the nick in her teeth from continually holding a needle or thread does point to her being an artisan of the court probably busily working in the industrial lower west ward. Is it possible that the predominantly male group of Scandinavian burials represents traders and seafearers? Some of these Scandinavian burials predate the fabled first recorded Viking raid on Holy Island in AD 793, so this adds much more nuance to the cosmopolitan nature of Bamburgh and it outward facing nature. And remarkably we have a skeleton that dates to about AD 650. It is that of a man who was 50 years old when he died in Bamburgh and his isotopes suggests he came from the western isles of Scotland – possibly Iona. So, this man was a direct contemporary of both Oswald and St Aidan, and it is completely reasonable to assume he travelled to Bamburgh with Oswald or Aidan in AD 634 or 635. That is a remarkable thing to be able to say, to make tangible links between archaeological evidence with the mystical lives of the great northern saints. This man, like many of the congregation, would have actually heard St Aidan preach with St Oswald translating.

So, in 2016, when all the research was complete Francis Armstrong, the owner of Bamburgh Castle along with the Bamburgh Research Project were starting to investigate the reburial of the Bowl Hole skeletons. The reburial of the excavated remains was a condition of the exhumation licence issued by the Ministry of Justice. There were several considerations – the Bowl Hole site is within the dynamic sand dunes which is not exactly the most stable conditions to dig a large trench, there is a likelihood of encountering more buried archaeological deposits, in addition the dunes have a wealth of natural environment designation that contributed to the decision not to rebury the remains from the vicinity from which they came. As stated above these were Christain burials and so should be buried in consecrated ground – the nearest being the graveyard surrounding St Aidan's church in the heart of the village.

Jude Aldred and Revd Brian Hurst during their initial interpretation visit to the crypt in October 2015
© J. Turner

Around the same time Bamburgh Heritage Trust were looking for a theme to illustrate the historic importance of Bamburgh and a small venue to start telling that story. The Revd Brian Hurst, vicar of St Aidan's Church at the time and the then chair of Bamburgh Heritage Trust suggested the group consider the crypt of the church as a possible venue. The crypt below the chancel had an old treacherous external stone staircase which about thirty years previously resulted in a broken ankle for a parishioner and the decision was taken not to use the space regularly. So, the crypt became a repository of a few chairs and various curios but was not serving an ecclesiastical function. The crypt comprises of two rooms, entry is into the first bigger room that covers about two-thirds of the space, with a beautiful double vaulted ceiling and stone slabbed floor. Immediately opposite the entrance is a curious small 1m by 1m access hole into the second crypt occupying the remaining third of the total space. A single small window at the east end is the only illumination for the narrow space which still retains an earth floor.

It is difficult to be certain when or who suggested the idea of creating an ossuary for the Bowl Hole skeletons in the second crypt, but it was quickly agreed to be a fitting solution for the interpretation aspirations of BHT and the reburial options for BRP and the Castle.

Bamburgh Heritage Trust successfully secured funding from the Coastal Community Revival Fund and set about creating the actual ossuary in the crypt. Being mindful of the sensitivities of the church of England but also the fragile condition of the bones the creation of an ossuary similar to some of the more ornamental ones on the continent with walls festooned with fans of femurs and circles of mandibles was not practical or appropriate. So, inspiration came from modern charnelling practices to place the bones into individual boxes. Needless to say it is impossible to source ossuary boxes in the United Kingdom so the 110 charnel boxes were ordered from Italy with Sally Whitton, a dual resident of Bamburgh and Lucca, acting as the intermediary for the sale. The zinc boxes came from a firm called Ceabis who specialise in medical, mortuary and funerary products.

It was incredibly important to all involved that it was clearly understood and articulated that creation of the ossuary was as the final resting place for the Bowl Hole skeletons. The ossuary was not created to allow easy access to the bone assemblage. The bones interment in the crypt is no different to a burial in the cemetery. The skeletons were placed in the crypt because they are such a remarkable congregation, and because of their close connection to both St Aidan and St Oswald. It is astounding to be able to make tangible links that the community of Bamburgh are rightly proud of their Anglo-Saxon ancestors and felt that the final destination in their posthumous journey should be equal to the endeavour and significance.

Grille detail showing the dragons head lock
© Andy Gardner Web Design

The reinterment in the crypt is their final resting place and they cannot be disturbed – only a Faculty from the church authority would enable the reopening of a single box and there is little conceivable reason for any such Faculty to be granted. It is incredibly fitting that the Bowl Hole congregation rest in peace in the crypt on the site of St Aidan's first Northumberian church where they heard him preach.

To ensure the sanctity of the ossuary Bamburgh Heritage Trust commissioned local blacksmith and artist Stephen Lunn to create a grille to secure the access between the two crypts. From his fascinating forge in Red Row some 30 miles south of Bamburgh, Stephen created a number of designs. The final grille is a beautiful three-dimensional reimagining and merging of the Celtic zoomorphic tradition with Anglo-Saxon inspired knot work. The grille enables the zinc ossuary boxes to be glimpsed whilst reminding the observer of the remarkable early Medieval origins of the people interred behind it.

Grille and Ossuary
© I. Glendinning

The Ceremony

On Friday 24th June 2016 one hundred and ten ossuary boxes were interred to their final resting place in the crypt in a ceremony performed by the Archdeacon of Lindisfarne Peter Robinson and Revd Brian Hurst. It was an extraordinary event. The day before 100 zinc boxes were transferred from the castle by a willing group of volunteers and placed into the crypt. On the Friday the undertakers Go As You Please collected the remaining 10 boxes in a beautiful horse drawn hearse from the castle followed on foot by the archaeologists from Bamburgh Research Project. Hundreds of people attended the service to hear the historian and author Max Adams and archaeologist Graeme Young from Bamburgh Research Project both speak about the archaeological and historic significance of the congregation and the time they lived. The poem *The Seafarer* and the Lord's Prayer were read in Old English – the language of the Anglo-Saxons that was strangely foreign but at the same time as familiar in tone and rhythm as today's speech. It was an extraordinary enough feat to be interring Anglo-Saxon skeletons but, as Max Adams pointed out, all the more extraordinary that we were celebrating and honouring a pan-European population on the very day that we, as a nation, found out the result of the national referendum on Britain's relationship with the European Union and that we, as a nation, had chosen to go it alone. Whichever way people had voted it certainly meant that an already significant day was charged with a palpable emotion.

The interment ceremony
© I. Glendinning

*Ten ossuary boxes are received into the church by Revd Briain Hurst and
Archdeacon Peter Robinson with Jude Aldred behind
© I. Glendinning*

*Right and below:
Interment ceremony in the church prior to
the ten boxes joining the hundred already
placed in the crypt
© I. Glendinning*

Opening the crypt to the public

It took over two years from the creation of the ossuary to opening it officially to the public. This was only made possible through a generous grant from the National Lottery Heritage Fund and a wonderful working partnership of Bamburgh Heritage Trust, St Aidan's Parochial Church Council, and the Northumberland Coast AONB Partnership supported by Graeme Young and Jo Kirton of Bamburgh Research Project and Professor Charlotte Roberts from Durham University.

It was during these two years that Revd Hurst moved south to a new parish and St Aidan's Church and Bamburgh were incredibly fortunate to have the Reverend Louise Taylor-Kenyon join them. Louise arrived as the project delivery started and has proved to be a brilliant and enthusiastic champion of the project as well as a much loved vicar for the

Access down to the crypt prior to the National Lottery Heritage Funding © J. Turner

Access down to the crypt after the National Lottery Heritage Funding © J. Turner

Access up from the crypt prior to the National Lottery Heritage Funding © J. Turner

Access up from the crypt after the National Lottery Heritage Funding © J. Turner

Bamburgh, Belford and Lucker communities. And sadly, it was towards the end of this two year period that Jude Aldred died. The completion of this project is her legacy.

The collective endeavour of the creative and brilliant minds of some amazing consultants and contractors resulted in the beautiful interpretation in the crypt and church, the safe access to the crypt, the new platform, the digital projection, the touchscreens, the online ossuary and website which ultimately enabled everyone to access Aidan – his story and that of his congregation. This is the first new early medieval ossuary in Britain and the first digital ossuary. Special mention and thanks must go to Kate McHughs and the unflappable Adam Fisher of Bright 3D, Jo Scott, Katherine Williams and Andy and James Gardner.

The crypt was officially opened on 21st November 2019 by the Bishop of Newcastle, the Right Reverend Christine Hardman supported by the Archdeacon of Lindisfarne, the Venerable Peter Robinson and Bamburgh's vicar the Revd Louise Taylor-Kenyon.

Interpretation © R. Turner

Revd Louise Taylor-Kenyon
© Crest

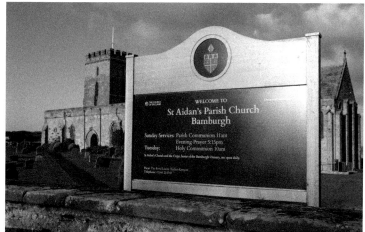

*Christine Hardman, the Bishop of Newcastle,
blessing the opening of the crypt © Crest*

*Congregation gathered for the blessing of the crypt
© A. Fisher*

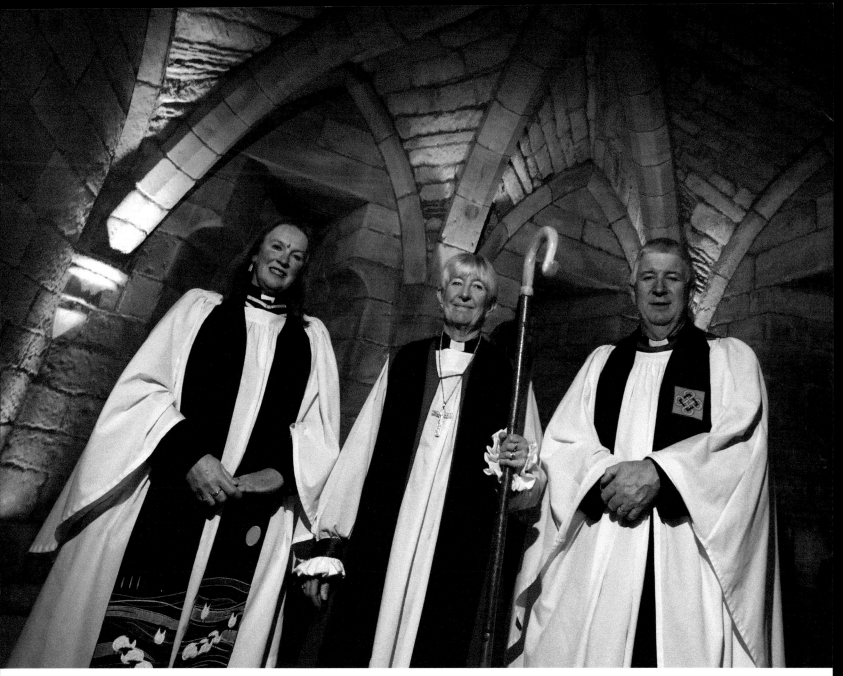

Revd Louise Taylor-Kenyon, Bishop Christine and Archdeacon Peter Robinson
© Crest

With the support of volunteers the crypt is open daily from around 10am – 5pm.

Owain Kirby Illustration

The interpretation in the crypt centres on the amazing lino-cut illustration by the artist Owain Kirby. Simple animation of details within each image bring the story to life. These three images represent Bamburgh through time from the Anglo-Saxon period to today and are an integral part of the projection in the crypt. The film, with sub titles, is also available on the touch screens at the back of the church.

Digital Ossuary

The digital ossuary, available online at bamburghbones.org and on the touchscreens at the rear of the church, contains the records for every identifiable individual excavated from the Bowl Hole cemetery. There are 98 records available and it is possible to filter the entries to discover where they came from, their aliments, age, and lives. Each record contains a photograph, drawing and map of their location in the cemetery.

Everyone in the ossuary was a living breathing person – they all had lives and names but there is no way of knowing their names. These were people, not just data so whilst it did not seem appropriate to rename them, each entry was given a codeword instead to help differentiate individuals. The codewords were randomly assigned and the etymology of each word is fascinating.

St Aidan illustrations by Sir Frank William Brangwyn

The beautiful front cover depicting *St Aidan, Bishop of Northumbria, A.D. 635, training boys at Lindisfarne* and *The death of St Aidan* sketch on page 105 are works by one of the most influential artists of the 19th and 20th centuries Sir Frank Brangwyn (1867–1956).

Sir Frank Brangwyn was a fabulously prolific artist, it is estimated that he produced over 12,000 works in various media – painting, sketches, etchings, wood cuts, mosaic, and murals together with furniture and stained glass. He designed whole rooms, building exteriors and even the decorations for Pacific liners. During his lifetime Brangwyn was incredibly popular and celebrated on the continent, but his slightly fractious relationship with the British art establishment might have tempered his popularity at home. He was made a full member of the Royal Academy in 1919 and knighted in 1941.

Guillaume Francois (known as Frank) Brangwyn was born in Bruges, Belgium in 1867 during his father's tenure as the designer of a parish church for the Belgian Guild of St Thomas and St Luke. The family returned to Britain when Brangwyn was around the age of seven or eight. It appears that Brangwyn did not flourish through formal education but rather developed an eye for architecture, crafts, and art through his father's work and by immersing himself in the vibrant London streetscape. Remarkably by the age of about 16 Brangwyn was apprenticed to the workshop of William Morris – where he learnt a variety of artistic techniques such as murals, glass, furniture, and painting and began to develop as a complete designer.

The fabulous *St Aidan, Bishop of Northumbria, A.D. 635, training boys at Lindisfarne* that graces the front cover of this book is part of a series of murals produced for the chapel of Christ's Hospital School in Horsham. The commission dates from 1912-1923 and came about as part of Brangwyn's close association with architects Webb and Bell. The commission consisted of sixteen panels illustrating *The Mission and Expansion of Christianity, beginning with the Acts of the Apostles and leading to the Conversion of our own Islands, and Foreign Missionary Work.* The painted tempera murals on gesso ground, measuring c2.5m by 2.2m were designed to fill the "gloomy brick void" between the top of the tiered stalls and the high windows of the chapel. There is no doubt that the frescos give the space a beautiful luminosity. The different scenes are so varied and contain such intricate and beautiful details that any congregation sitting below must surely be absorbed and inspired. Other themes depicted include *St. Augustine landing at Ebbsfleet*, *St. Columba arriving on Iona*, *St. Wilfrid teaching the South Saxons* and *The Martyrdom of St. Alban*.

The mural at Christ's Hospital is not the only depiction of St Aidan that Brangwyn did – between 1910-1916 he created the mosaic around the apse of St Aidan's Church in Leeds. The mosaic depicts four periods in Aidan's life - feeding the poor, his arrival at Lindisfarne, preaching and on his deathbed. The sketch is a preparatory cartoon for the final mosaic.

Whilst much of Brangwyn's work focuses on the secular – some of his favourite subjects being ship building, factory workers and industry – his religious pieces are full of beautiful, dignified pathos. It seems incredibly appropriate that Brangwyn should depict St Aidan, surely there is a parallel between Aidan's preaching of equality of all people and living things and Brangwyn's socialism and belief that art should not be restricted to the privileged few.

For more information about Brangwyn and the Christ's Hospital murals there is an excellent book by Dr. Libby Horner, as well as postcards of the murals and cartoon drawings, available from the Christ's Hospital Museum website. It is possible to view the murals by appointment and this can be arranged by contacting the museum direct.

The image of 'St Aidan, Bishop of Northumbria, A.D. 635, training boys at Lindisfarne' has been reproduced here by the kind permission of David Brangwyn and Christ's Hospital.

Brangwyn's efficient use and reuse characters and studies might help explain his prolific output. The figure of 'A Young Girl with Red Hair (right) appears in the same pose in panel 1 *'St. Peter Standing Up with the Eleven'* at Christ's Hospital and is depicted again at St.Aidan's, Leeds where she is rendered in mosaic as opposed to paint, and is centrally placed the third event – St. Aidan preaching - of the four themes depicting the life of the saint.

The characterful 'boy' on the far left of the teaching mural is also evident in at the side of the preaching section of the Leeds mosaic.

Reproduced here by kind permission of Christ's Hospital

Acknowledgements

National Lottery Heritage Fund – in particular Sara Sproates, our project officer

Other funders: Community Foundation, The Barbour Foundation, The Joicey Trust, Sir James Knott Trust, Garfield Weston, Northumberland Coast AONB Partnership, Northumberland County Council, Cllr Guy Renner-Thompson

Professor Charlotte Roberts -Durham University,

Jo Kirton and Graeme Young Bamburgh Research Project

All of Bamburgh Heritage Trust (past and present) – Sam Morton, Colin Brunt, John Woodman, Susie Dodds, Chris Baldwin, Carol Griffiths, Sally Whitton, Bill Hindmarsh, Susan Shanks, Sue Aldred and Noel Page

St Aidan's Church and the Parochial Church Council – Revd Lousie Taylor-Kenyon, Revd Brian Hurst, Sheila Bacon, Pauline Lees, Peter and Evelyn Elliot, Gill Bardgett, Linda Kirby, Charles Baker-Creswell, and all of the PCC

Volunteers and community – Kate and Meg Morton, Karen and John Lamb, TG, Francesca Burke, Mary Dixon, Robert Mckibbin, Alex Lorraine, Valerie Glass, Gerldine Terry, Jo Tilsley, Sue Raynor, Graham Davison, Susan Parker, Martin Harvey, Michael Gibson, Jacqueline Molloy, Patrick Cordingly and Christine Chapman. Rob, Gilbert and Edmund Turner and Roisin and Vincent Cowley

Contractors – Katherine Williams, Kate McHughs and Adam Fisher at Bright 3D, Jo Scott, Craig at Pixel Stag, Wavetech, Elmwood, Elizabeth Baker, Andy and James Gardner of Adam Gardner Web Design, Dan Hedley, Richard Carlton and Peter Ryder from Archaeological Practice, Linda Bankier at Berwick Archive

The Armstrong family and all the staff at Bamburgh Castle. Staff and volunteers at the Grace Darling museum

Northumberland Coast AONB Partnership staff team– Catherine Grey, Iain Robson, Sarah Winlow, and David Feige

Academic steering group: Professor Claire Lees, Dr. John Challis, Dr Tony Williams

Funders:

Made possible with
Heritage Fund

Garfield Weston
FOUNDATION

SIR JAMES KNOTT TRUST

The Joicey Trust

Community Foundation

Northumberland
County Council

THE
Barbour
FOUNDATION

Project Partners:

NORTHUMBERLAND COAST
AREA OF OUTSTANDING NATURAL BEAUTY

BAMBURGH
HERITAGE TRUST

BAMBURGH
Research Project

Durham
University

THE CHURCH
OF ENGLAND
Diocese of Newcastle

The Parish Church of
Saint Aidan
Bamburgh